Glass House

Nicky Adams

Glass House

Buildings for Open Living

The Vendome Press
New York

First published in the United States of America in 2008 by
The Vendome Press
1334 York Avenue
New York, NY 10021

Created and produced for The Vendome Press by
Palazzo Editions Ltd,
15 Gay Street, Bath, BA1 2PH, UK
www.palazzoeditions.com

Book design: Bernard Higton
Picture research: Sue Ucel
Managing editor: Victoria Webb
Copy editor: Iona Baird

ISBN-13: 978-0-86565-190-6

Library of Congress Cataloging-in-Publication Data

Adams, Nicky.
  Glass house : buildings for open living / Nicky Adams.
      p. cm.
  ISBN 978-0-86565-190-6 (hardcover : alk. paper)
  1. Glass construction. 2. Architecture, Domestic. I. Title.
  NA7186.A33 2008
  721'.04496--dc22

                           2007029085

Printed in Singapore

First Printing

Page 2 Stupendous canyon views through the glass walls of Simpatico Sem, designed by Stephen H Kanner and perched on a hill in Malibu, California.

Right Light floods into the glazed gallery of a former Victorian stables in London, transformed into a modern glass home by architect Seth Stein in 1995.

Following pages The curved glass structures of this Californian home create a 'village of forms' according to its architect, Ed Niles.

Contents

Introduction

'Space and light and order. Those are the things that men need, just as much as they need bread or a place to sleep.' Le Corbusier knew full well when he wrote those words in 1923, in his hugely influential book *Vers une architecture*, that he and the mid-20th-century band of pioneers in residential architecture that followed closely behind were beginning to identify a new way of day-to-day living – one that required a reinvention of the place in which to do it.

The dream of Le Corbusier – which was taken up by Philip Johnson, Ludwig Mies van der Rohe, Pierre Koenig and many others who became influenced by the first stirrings of this new style – was for a more fluid, flexible and free space in which to live. The interior of the mid-20th-century modernist home could easily be translated into a more organic form, by the removal of conventional partition walls to create open spaces that flowed languorously from one to another. However, there was an even greater freedom to be found in replacing some of the outside walls with a material that was only just beginning to show itself as a practical and versatile building material – glass.

Throughout the dawning of the modernist age, glass technology was surging ahead with new ways to make glass clearer, tougher and more reliable as a building material that could take the place of traditional bricks, blocks or concrete. As architectural pioneers called for more transparency and less obscurity in their designs, glass manufacturers were able to provide for them panes in larger and more creative styles that responded to their growing aesthetic wants and needs. In an almost miraculous way, the boundaries for living all but disappeared. Divided physically by the merest membrane of near-invisible glass, the newly imagined free-flowing inside spaces were invited to spill outside, capturing, embracing and bringing in both landscape and light – and with them, life.

In the days, months and years that have passed since the first glass houses were envisaged, built, discussed, and then discussed some more, our way of living has undergone a gradual transformation of its own. While conventional homes with individual spaces for individual purposes are still designed, constructed and lived in happily around the world, there is also a strong undercurrent that pulls insistently towards the ideals of the 20th-century modernists. As life in the 21st century becomes less formalized in a variety of ways, and the importance of being relaxed in the home environment grows, houses are called upon to evolve to suit these ever-changing needs. Flexible, adaptable, open-plan living has become an achievement for many, and an aspiration for thousands more. Thanks to advances in glass technology even greater than Le Corbusier and his contemporaries ever dreamed possible, the opportunities for living in a house that is open to such an extent that it is to all intents and purposes a part of the outdoors are becoming more widespread. Although commissioning an architect-designed glass house is certainly beyond the means of many, the fact that some of the most successful aspects of glass-house design are now being absorbed into the construction of new homes – whether individual or mass produced – reflects a general yearning for homes that are light, bright and have expansive views.

The design of specially commissioned glass houses can vary greatly. Some are profoundly anchored in the seminal styles of the 20th-century pioneers, while others take their essential ideas and let them fly, creating palaces of sparkling translucency that are as much sculpture as shelter. If the architects rein themselves in sufficiently, the design of the glass house represents a direct response to the specific desires of the owner. It is no coincidence that some of the most striking buildings in this medium have been designed by architects for themselves.

Taking the idea of open-plan living to its natural conclusion, many glass houses are conceived as conduits for an indoor-outdoor style of living, where life flows naturally from the interior to the exterior and back again, without the tedium of lifting the latch of a window or turning the handle on a solid door. While this 'West Coast' lifestyle is particularly favoured in the world's warmer regions, the great thermal properties of modern glass, coupled with advances in engineering, make this a possibility in colder climes, too. Indoor swimming pools with the deep end in the garden are a favourite, especially if there is a glass roof that can be slid over the top if the weather turns chilly. Dining areas that can become al fresco at the touch of a button are also popular features of glass houses.

Glass's great gift to a house is undoubtedly light, and there are many tired-looking, neglected houses in desperate need of a ray of sunshine. Simply replacing a solid wall with a run of full-height glass windows or doors, or even just glazing a roof, can totally transform a home, changing it beyond all recognition.

Among the most triumphant glass houses are those that have been built to see, just as much as to be seen. Spectacularly scenic locations are the ideal situations for glass houses. Not only can they be designed not to impact unnecessarily on the beauty of the natural surroundings, they also make the very best of a good vantage point. Huge expanses of glass windows frame the vista of a rocky canyon, an impressive mountain range, a thick forest, a tranquil landscape, an ever-changing seascape or simply the serenity of an inner-city garden. These are glass houses whose insides are full of the outside.

Designed in different ways, in different settings, to suit different people, the glass houses of today give a fascinating insight into the way we live our lives and how, in doing so, we relate to our surroundings. As Le Corbusier predicted, space and light and order have become a very necessary part of the modern place to live.

Pierre Koenig pioneered the use of industrial materials to create aesthetically pleasing and simply built homes in 1950s California, including the elegant glass and steel Case Study 21.

Looking back at the work of some of the world's pioneering architects from the 20th century it is sometimes difficult to believe that their residential buildings date from a different era to our own. Their revolutionary use of glass – whether to harness light as a decorative feature, to blur the boundary between interior and exterior design, or as a direct replacement for bricks and mortar – has undeniably shaped a vast proportion of the domestic architecture built in their wake, and which fills the pages of this book with stunning, original and light-filled homes whose transparent need is to be lived in, enjoyed and loved.

The ancient Egyptians were the true innovators in the manufacture of glass. They discovered, unintentionally, that melting sand in a fire created a new and wondrously translucent material. Although the Egyptians soon learnt to fashion it into vases and drinking vessels, it was not until the Middle Ages that glass could be made into uniform pieces. The Venetians cornered the market in glass manufacture, and throughout the medieval period they travelled with their craft across Europe, where the brightly coloured glass pieces they produced were worked into intricate stained-glass windows to bring light, life and colour to the most magnificent cathedrals. Notre Dame, Aachen Cathedral, York Minster and many other Gothic masterpieces still stand testament to the skill of the stained-glass window makers.

Coloured and clear glass began to appear in the grander public buildings of Europe as well as the religious edifices of the time, but it was not until the Tudors came to the English throne that glass panes became sought-after for private houses. The high price of glass made it a valuable commodity, and the ostentatious Tudor aristocracy began to commission great homes, their façades crammed with the largest windows Venetian glass-manufacturing technology could create.

The glass and stone architecture of the Elizabethan period is perhaps the first indication that houses could, and would, be designed using glass as a building material in its own right. Many of the most impressive stately homes of this era – notably Hardwick Hall in Derbyshire and Worksop Manor, Nottinghamshire – still stand today and the fenestration never ceases to amaze. Panes of curved as well as flat glazing are configured in a way that is a marked departure from the idea of glass filling a hole in the wall to let in light. The windows represent a substantial proportion of the façade of these buildings and dominate the design style.

However, Tudor windows were generally composed of a collection of smaller panes, and it was not until plate-glass manufacturing became more successful that sizeable, single-pane windows could be produced. The French became expert in this, and it was to showcase the skill of the national plate-glass manufacturers that Louis XIV commissioned the great glazing of the Palace of Versailles. In 1678, J. H. Mansard trebled the palace's frontage and designed and installed a stunning series of floor-to-ceiling plate-glass windows, complemented by mirrors on the opposite wall, to flood the 73-metre (240-foot) long Hall of

Mirrors with light and create one of the palace's most impressive and beautiful rooms.

Versailles is widely regarded as the first glass house. It forged a link between the religious and public stone and glass structures of the Gothic age, and the industrial and commercial metal and glass buildings of the 19th century. These combined to inspire the groundbreaking architects of the 20th century, who set out to imagine a new way of living with glass.

Le Corbusier described the 1920s as a time when the window was battling to attain the greatest dimensions in the face of technical limitations, but when they did come, the technological advances that allowed the production of large sheets of glass had a profound effect on the evolution of modern architecture. New techniques in glass production created a material that was tough, versatile and beautiful, and those properties chimed with the revolution in residential architecture that was about to be unleashed.

For the innovative architects of the early 20th century, the use of large panes of glass symbolized the move away from solid, functional living spaces towards homes that were simply designed to empathize with their surroundings and to provide a fluid interior for a more open-plan style of living. The creativity, skill and tenacity of these innovators in designing the early contemporary glass houses is evident in the most iconic of their designs, a handful of which appear here, and all of which have gone on to influence the awe-inspiring glass houses of our own time.

UK: Chertsey, Surrey Describing it as 'a medium capable of endless adaptation without loss of integrity', Raymond McGrath was one of the first architects of the modernist period to become fascinated by the possibilities of glass in residential architecture.

An Australian of Irish descent, McGrath studied architecture at Sydney University before moving to England in 1926 to take up a fellowship at Clare College, Cambridge. While there, he was commissioned to carry out a bold remodelling of the interior of one of the college's Victorian houses, and McGrath saw this as an opportunity to experiment with the decorative use of glass, famously cladding the ceilings completely in mirrors.

McGrath's interest in the uses of glass for decorative effect led to his writing several articles on the subject, as well as a highly influential book, *Glass in Architecture and Decoration*, which was published in 1937. In it, McGrath embraced the use of glass in contemporary homes and identified 'the recent purge or spring-cleaning of architecture and design' that it heralded.

Nowhere is this 'spring clean' more evident than in the design of McGrath's first major project, a drum of an Art Deco house, which was built in 1937 for the landscape architect Christopher Tunnard and his partner G. L. Schlesinger. Set on a hillside plot in Chertsey, Surrey, McGrath described Hill House as 'my most ambitious piece of domestic architecture in England, looking like a

'A drum of an Art Deco house'

Left Built in 1936, this Modernist circular home by Raymond McGrath was described by the architect as 'a big round cheese with a slice cut out of it'.

Right The sweep of floor-to-ceiling windows at Hill House welcomes in the gardens, which were originally designed by the landscape architect Christopher Tunnard, for whom the house was built.

big round cheese with a slice cut out of it, facing south for the sunlight to enter'.

No doubt McGrath was inspired by the 18th-century gardens already well established on the plot, as Hill House is one of the first homes to have a spectacular curved glazed reception room, which offers a wonderfully panoramic view. The twelve full-height, metal-framed windows form a smooth, sweeping arc and create a living area that is the hub of the house. Upstairs, too, a bank of tall windows wraps around the master bedroom and gives an impressive view from a higher vantage point.

After a series of less-than-careful owners, the building – nicknamed 'big, round house' – fell into disrepair, until a new family bought it in 2000 and commissioned the architectural practice Munkenbeck+Marshall to restore their home to its modernist glory. With the metal frames of the huge windows now replaced, the Grade II-listed house is today a comfortable family home. Its glazed reception room has been much replicated since in contemporary homes and reflects perfectly the change to a more flexible, open way of living that McGrath correctly predicted would be the norm in the century to come.

Left The arc of the house is echoed in the hallway, where the curve of the staircase is reflected in vast mirrors.

Above Light floods the main living areas.

Right Upstairs, the shape of the house is accentuated by more curving windows in the master suite.

US: New Canaan, Connecticut 'This is the purest time that I ever had in my life to do architecture,' wrote Philip Johnson of his Glass House, completed in 1949. 'Everything else is tainted with the three problems: clients, function, and money. Here I had none of the three.'

In fact, Johnson's Glass House is fêted as one of the most beautiful – though least functional – homes ever built. Taking its inspiration from the work of celebrated modernist Ludwig Mies van der Rohe, Johnson's Glass House in New Canaan, Connecticut, is totally glass, with no solid walls at all.

Johnson is credited with bringing the modernism of European architects, including Mies van der Rohe and Le Corbusier, to America. As the first director of the department of architecture at New York's Museum of Modern Art, Johnson is believed to have coined the phrase 'the International Style' to describe the European modernism that was gradually coming to influence architecture around the world. In 1940 he returned to Harvard University to study architecture under Marcel Breuer, and it was while preparing his thesis for his masters degree that he designed the Glass House for himself.

Its design was certainly a radical departure from traditional North American residential architecture. Supported by a grey steel frame, the house sits squarely in the landscape – and with no internal walls to touch the glass exterior, it is essentially a glass box. Inside is just one room, divided into areas for living and sleeping by low walnut cabinets. A brick cylinder contains the bathroom.

Built for beauty rather than function, Johnson imagined the Glass House more as a statement on design than as a place to live. However, unlike the even more emphatically minimalist designs that followed, it has a symmetry and solidity that still relates it to the accepted traditions of residential architecture. It marked the start of Johnson's fifty-year odyssey of experimentation in forms, materials and ideas. The results of this are the many 'pavilions' that pepper 16 hectares (40 acres) of Connecticut and which earned Johnson the first Pritzker Architecture Prize, presented in 1979.

In 1986, Johnson handed the Glass House over to the US National Trust and in 2007, two years after the architect's death, the house was opened to the public, who visit to admire the purity of one of the world's first and most iconic glass houses.

'One of the world's first and most iconic glass houses'

Left The interior of Johnson's Glass House is essentially just one room, a flowing space dominated by views of the landscape through its glass walls.

Right More a statement on design than a place to live, the house is purely of glass, with no internal walls to mar the transparent exterior.

'A simple transparent glass rectangle'

US: Plano, Illinois 'I pointed out to Mies that a glass house was impossible because you had to have rooms, and that meant solid walls up against the glass, which ruined the whole point,' said Philip Johnson at a symposium held at Columbia University in 1961. 'Mies said, "I think it can be done".'

While Johnson's solution to the difficulty of creating a house completely of glass was to replace the internal walls with furniture, his contemporary, Ludwig Mies van der Rohe, took the idea further. The Farnsworth House, near Plano, Illinois, was built in 1951 and is one of the most radically minimalist houses ever designed. A simple glass rectangle, its interior is totally open-plan except for a small rectangular structure that contains two bathrooms and a kitchen. Other than this, it is almost completely transparent.

Mies is one of the most iconic of the modernist architects. Born in Aachen in 1886, he served his apprenticeship in Germany and designed several projects for glass skyscrapers in Berlin in the 1920s. For the Barcelona World Exposition in 1929 he designed a

pavilion for the Germans, known as the Barcelona Pavilion - a simple, rectangular glass structure that set a precedent for much of his later work. Mies was director of the Dessau Bauhaus for three years until its closure in 1933, and four years later he moved to America, where he became a significant force for architectural change in the post-Second World War rebuilding period.

Mies saw art in the functional steel frame of mass construction, and brought a touch of classicism to the large volumes of the many American public buildings he was commissioned to design. He is best known for his towering symbols of American commercialism, including the stunning glass and steel Seagram Building in New York, built in 1958 as a collaboration with Philip Johnson.

However, Mies also designed a handful of residential buildings, including, in 1951, the Farnsworth House, created as a country retreat for Dr Edith Farnsworth on a plot of land overlooking the Fox River.

In fact, the house is more building than residential, and there

has been much debate since its construction about its suitability as a place to live. It is a dwelling in its simplest form - a glass box, raised 1.5 metres (5 feet) off the ground, aloof from its lush setting and also from the general paraphernalia associated with everyday habitation. White steel columns support the planar levels of the floor and the roof of the one-storey building, and the inside space flows freely without the encumbrance of excessive furniture or possessions. The seamless glass sides expose every aspect of life within, and the leafy surroundings offer the only privacy.

Marking a turning point in domestic architecture, Mies van der Rohe's Farnsworth House stands as a stunning example of simple aesthetics transcending the accepted requirements for everyday living.

Left Mies' glass box in a leafy Illinois setting is an icon of international style modernism. The façade is composed of single panes of glass spanning floor to ceiling and fastened to the structural system by steel mullions.

Below Eight steel columns give structure to a pure glass prism, which is raised 15 metres off the ground on steel stilts.

Left The glass walls ensure that the house is open to the landscape on all sides.

Below Continuous visual space is the essence of the house, which is totally undivided save for the rectangular bathroom and kitchen enclosure.

Right The flowing interior of The Farnsworth House is unencumbered by the clutter of everyday living, with even the necessary furniture kept to an absolute minimum.

US: Hollywood Hills, California Taking a step on from the purity of Mies van der Rohe's Farnsworth House and Philip Johnson's Glass House, Pierre Koenig's Case Study designs set out to bring an element of practicality to elegant modern living.

Hailed as one of the great American modernists of the post-war period, Koenig was preoccupied with the notion of taking materials that were hitherto considered only suitable for industrial use and translating them into a residential setting. 'Industry has not learned the difference between what is beautiful in its simplicity and what is ugly although equally simple,' Koenig is quoted as saying.

In 1956, four years after graduating from the University of Southern California in Los Angeles, Koenig got his chance to prove that functional yet aesthetically appealing houses could be constructed from the simplest industrial materials. Having designed and built a small steel-framed prototype home of his own, he was asked to contribute two designs to the series of Case Study Houses, an initiative sponsored by *Arts & Architecture* magazine that called for the major architects of the day to help

'An elegant and unadorned edifice of glass and steel'

Above True to Koenig's conviction that standard structural parts could be used in a limitless number of permutations to build practical homes, the Bailey House is constructed of a series of factory-made steel-framed boxes, which were assembled on-site.

Right The great, industrial-sized glass panels are reflected in the pools that surround the house.

Above The living room has full-height glass sliding doors that open onto a terraced entertaining area.

solve the housing shortage caused by the return of soldiers from the Second World War.

Along with such names as Richard Neutra, Craig Ellwood, Eero Saarinen, and Charles and Ray Eames, Koenig was challenged to create a home that would be efficient to run and cheap to build in large numbers. In the final event, 36 houses in the series were designed between 1945 and 1966, and built in Los Angeles and the San Francisco Bay Area. Koenig built two, numbers 21 and 22, both elegant and unadorned edifices of glass and steel that allowed the architect to showcase his notion of giving natural expression to the industrial materials that were in plentiful supply.

Case Study 21, or Bailey House, is set on a level site in the Hollywood hills, and consists of a series of standard steel-framed boxes, welded together and entirely glazed on two sides to take in the valley views to the north and south and to reveal the fluidity of this modern home. The entrance is through a 9-metre (30-foot) carport, which opens directly into the foyer and then flows into the living room and out through the glass doors into the garden on the south side. The bedrooms and bathrooms are set in the western wing of the house, facing a central courtyard and fountain. The great glazed sides are reflected in the many pools of water that surround the house.

Koenig's visionary approach to the use of glass and steel in residential building has been inspirational to the long list of celebrated architects who have followed him in his quest for simplicity of design and efficiency of construction. His influence can be seen in many of the most elegant glass houses of the late 20th and early 21st centuries.

Below The two bedrooms and two bathrooms are housed in the western wing and open out onto the central courtyard.

Australia: Wahroonga, New South Wales Although this house, by Viennese-born architect Harry Seidler, has provided a talking point for architects since it was designed in 1948, it is itself influenced by the Bauhaus movement of the 1920s. Seidler studied architecture in America under the founder of the Bauhaus school of design, Walter Gropius, and was also taught by renowned Bauhaus devotees Joseph Albers and Marcel Breuer. On finishing his studies, Seidler left New York for Australia and started work on his first commission, a house for his parents on a 2.6-hectare (6.4-acre) patch of bushland in Wahroonga, New South Wales.

Embracing the concepts of space, artistic abstraction and new technologies espoused by the Bauhaus, Seidler created a rectangular, spectacularly glazed home, hollowed out on all sides, that would invite a relationship between the interior and the exterior. Set in the middle of the plot rather than at the edge – as was the convention of the time – Seidler considered the house to be a part of its surroundings, allowing the natural landscape to become a feature of the interior, and also to lend it much-needed privacy.

Named after the architect's mother, the completed Rose Seidler House has a definite sculptural quality, true to the Bauhaus philosophy of uniting art with architecture. Designed as a cube, with a section removed at the bottom and another cut from the centre, the house has no solid walls; its plate-glass sides make it

Right The sculptural quality of the Rose Seidler House demonstrates Seidler's Bauhaus influences.

Below The flowing interior of the house has been furnished in authentic 1950s style, with pieces by Eames, Saarinen and Hardoy, by the Historic Houses Trust of New South Wales.

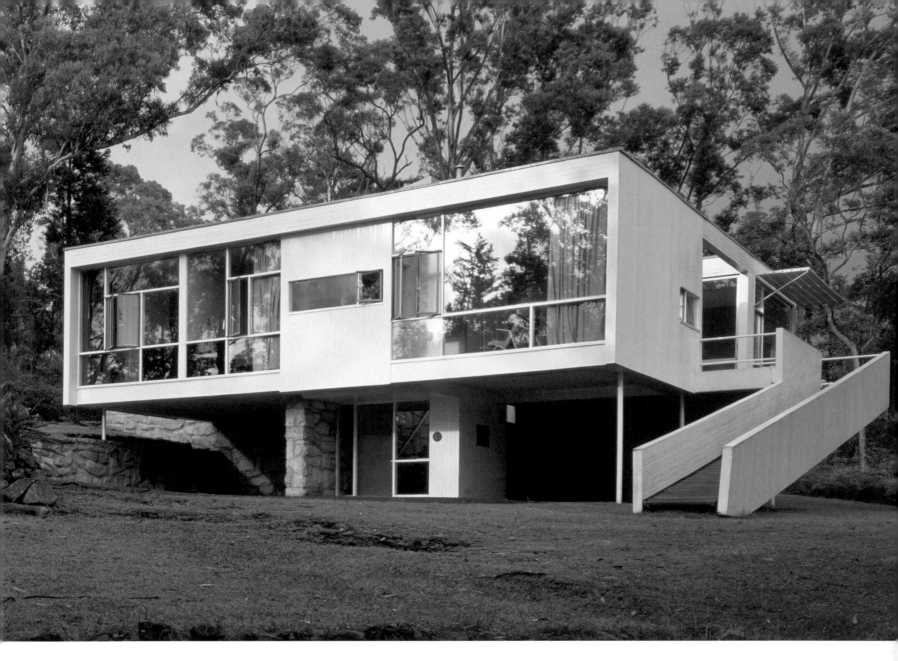

'Plate-glass sides make it appear to float just above the ground'

appear to float just above the ground, only tethered by a louvre screen, a ramp and a stone wall. The square bite from the middle of the cube forms a sun deck, next to which is a two-storey-high well, which pierces into the building vertically, flooding with light the otherwise rather dark centre.

The interior of the house is an exercise in the new notion of open-plan living. A central family room is the link between the living and sleeping accommodation and the rest of the house. Divided from both sides only by curtains, the inner space can be left open to allow the house to flow freely from one area to another. Pulling across one set of curtains adds the space to one

side or the other, and pulling both sets creates a self-contained room in the middle, separating the two wings of the house.

Awarded the Sulman Medal in 1952, Rose Seidler House introduced many new concepts in residential architecture, including the use of glass as a functional as well as aesthetic building material.

Seidler's parents lived in the house until 1967 and, in 1988, it was acquired by the Historic Houses Trust of New South Wales and opened to the public in its authentic 1950s condition, furnished with pieces by important post-war designers including Eames, Saarinen and Hardoy.

UK: East Grinstead, Surrey With very obvious references to the Californian Case Study programme, Space House is a British design classic. Still fresh and futuristic-looking today, it was built in 1963–64 by the architects Peter Foggo and David Thomas, who went on to greater fame at Arup Associates. In the early 1960s, however, the two men were recent graduates with an architecture practice, run as a sideline in the evenings and at weekends.

Space House, in the perhaps unlikely setting of East Grinstead, Surrey, was one of only a handful of buildings designed by Foggo and Thomas under their own banner, and was conceived as a prototype for the housing of the future. Taking the Case Studies as its influence, the house is a glazed, steel-framed H-shape. Living accommodation is provided in one of the long sections, with bedrooms in the other. The central connecting bar contains a kitchen, a bathroom and a utility room.

The symmetry of the design is accentuated to great effect by the dramatic floor-to-ceiling glazing, which allows the house's mature gardens to spill in on all sides. The most striking feature,

'A prototype for the housing of the future'

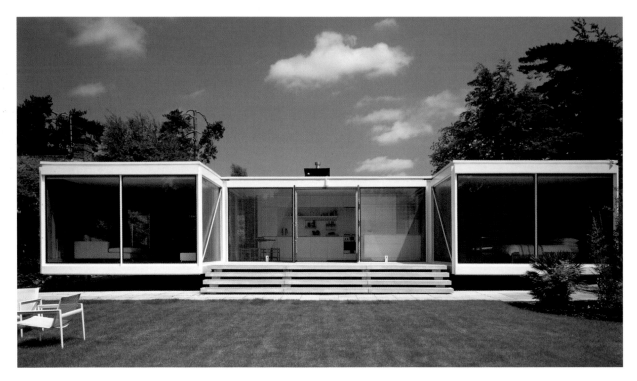

Left and above The futuristic design of Space House belies the fact that it was built in the mid-1960s. Essentially a glass H-shape, the extensive glazed perimeter allows light to flood in on all sides.

Below Restoration in 2004 by
Lee/Fitzgerald, in which the steel
frame was painted a bright white, has
revived the house and turned it into a
practical, modern family home.

though, is the open-plan living section - nearly 15 metres (50 feet) of fluid, glazed space that serves as a place for living, dining and study all in one.

More than forty years after its original construction, the house is still a workable family home. A successful programme of refurbishment, instigated by the new owners of the house and carried out by architects Lee/Fitzgerald, has successfully and subtly updated the house for modern living. Where once the steel frame of the house was black, it is now white, adding to the

property's futuristic appeal. The terraced sun deck, added in the void on one side of the H, offers a similar attraction. At the same time, several internal doors have been removed to improve the flow of the house, and two bedrooms were knocked into one to enhance the open-plan style.

The RIBA judged the changes to be so in keeping with the original ethos of this - one of the UK's most influential glass houses - that in 2004 Space House received the Association's award for conservation.

Right The interior of the house is
flooded with light from the great glass
windows, and since restoration is even
more open-plan than the architects
originally envisaged.

UK: Wimbledon, London Described by Richard Rogers as 'a transparent tube with solid boundary walls', this innovative glass house represented British Architecture at the 1967 Paris Biennale and is still a landmark design.

Commissioned by Rogers's parents, it is set on a long, narrow wooded plot, opposite Wimbledon Common and on a major road. The house consists of two glass-sided and glass-topped oblongs, cleverly arranged for maximum privacy in this urban spot. The

smaller of the two units, which houses a flat and a pottery studio, is set closest to the road and successfully buffers the noise of urban life for the principal wing of the house, which comprises the main accommodation. Both rectangles overlook a secluded central courtyard garden, which provides an oasis of calm.

The steel frame of the house is demountable, while the internal partition walls are also moveable. The eight welded-steel portals are set in the interior of the two glass-shelled buildings, both for

Above This glass house was commissioned by Rogers' parents in 1968 and is characterised by its maximum sized, double-glazed, sealed units in painted steel frames with glazed roofs.

'Innovative design meets modern living'

elegance and with the practical intention of facilitating the joins between metal and glass and reducing maintenance.

Although designed in the 1960s, Dr Rogers' House references the elegant aesthetics as well as the obvious functionality of the 1940s Case Study designs of Pierre Koenig. The industrial steel-framed structure of the house is displayed through the plate glass by way of admiration rather than apology, and the open-plan design is as pleasing as it is practical. In this way, the house marks a point of transition between the innovative design concepts of the early glass houses and the creation of beautiful, practical and desirable glass houses suited to modern living in the late 20th and early 21st centuries.

Left The interior of the house is dominated by views of the lush garden that protects it from the hurly-burly of its urban setting.

Above Designed to provide maximum privacy, the house consists of two separate glazed oblongs facing an internal garden courtyard.

This stunning house in São Paulo,
Brazil, by celebrated contemporary
architect Marcio Kogan, is a prime
example of the use of glass coupled
with sophisticated engineering to open
up homes to their environments and
allow for the much-craved indoor-
outdoor lifestyle.

2 Indoor-Outdoor Living

Born out of a philosophical need to maintain a constant connection with the landscape, Asian architecture has a long and highly revered tradition of indoor-outdoor buildings. Although he rarely revealed his influences, the great early 20th-century innovator Frank Lloyd Wright is believed to have taken inspiration from Japanese architecture, in particular when developing his highly influential Prairie-style houses in northern California. These designs are widely considered to represent the first stirrings of indigenous American architecture and, as such, have had a profound effect on modern building design around the globe.

The typical Prairie house was long and low, often with a rambling and open-plan interior. Wright's designs were characterized by an abundance of windows, frequently arranged in banks, sometimes joining together so many panes that whole walls of glass were formed. A great exponent of the use of glass in residential architecture, Wright recognized that adding large windows allowed a close interaction between indoors and out that chimed with his passion for a new style of organic architecture, in which the building could be seen to evolve naturally from its context. In fact, in 1928, Wright wrote an essay equating glass with the mirrors of nature, such as lakes, rivers and ponds.

Much of suburban America's post-war architecture has its roots in Wright's Prairie design which, by the mid-20th century, had become absorbed into the typical single-storey informal New World home that can be seen today not just in the United States, but also in Canada, Australia, New Zealand and South Africa. However, modern advances in glass technology now allow for ever bigger, stronger panes of glass that harness dramatic views of the surrounding landscape and offer myriad possibilities for actually opening up the house to its surroundings, allowing indoors and outdoors to flow seamlessly together. Today – a century after Frank Lloyd Wright first proposed his ideals for an organic style of architecture – this blurring of the boundary between the interior and the exterior has become the preoccupation of the architects and owners of glass houses the world over.

'Southern California living: inside-out'

US: Pacific Palisades, California This geometrically intriguing glass home was built by the Santa Monica-based architect Stephen H. Kanner for his own family, to take advantage of the bright light and cool breezes in Pacific Palisades.

'The 511 house is about Southern California living: inside-out,' says Kanner. 'Before designing it, I asked myself, "How can a typical lot be utilized to make it seem larger and more open?" The result is a house that's all about lifestyle, not just another home with a contemporary façade.'

The modernist aesthetic of 511 House takes its inspiration from neighbouring buildings by Richard Neutra and Charles and Ray Eames, but the decision to use glass as the dominant material was as much practical as it was artistic. The long, narrow site – no bigger than a tennis court – could easily have enticed the architect into designing a dark and gloomy home, but Kanner triumphed over the limitations of the plot by pushing the house right to the boundary to maximize the outside space, and by incorporating into the design a generous amount of sparkling glass. 'The expansive glazing greedily collects natural light,' Kanner explains. 'It also brings in the crystalline skies, and the vast operable windows allow for cross-ventilation that cools the house in a passive way.'

Left The intriguing design of 511 House is a great showcase for the structural qualities of glass.

Below An exercise in geometry, the house sparkles with shiny floors, white-painted walls and crystalline glass.

Above and above right Glass panes light the house at all levels, while the circular bathroom mirror echoes the porthole window.

Right Sliding doors in the main living area open the house to its private garden and the cooling sea breezes.

Two sets of great glazed doors on the ground floor, measuring 2.4 x 2.4 metres (8 x 8 feet) and 2.4 x 2.5 metres (8 x 8.5 feet), simply slide open to bring the outside in, and vice versa, connecting the home with its own private garden, water sculpture and patio, which doubles as the children's play area. 'The landscaping was critical,' says Kanner, 'because it was the key to creating a private world.'

On the second storey, expanses of window and the angular jutting of the end wall make a design statement, while at the same time providing a unique vantage point over the neighbourhood. To protect the owner's privacy, however, the property is screened with timber bamboo, black bamboo and ficus hedges in front of horizontally slatted cedar fencing.

'The connection between the interior of the home and the natural site was important to my family,' says Kanner. 'The large sliding glass doors just disappear – along with the distinction between inside and outside – and provide a conduit for the soothing southern Californian sea breezes.'

US: Montecito, California 'Californian "Modernism" is very different from European "Modernism" in its preoccupation with the relationship of house to site,' says architect Barton Myers. 'In particular, due to our mild climate, the indoor-outdoor relationship is inspired by, of course, Japanese architecture.'

This was certainly uppermost in the architect's mind when he designed his own family home, Toro Canyon, to encompass its picturesque mountainous setting in Montecito, California. 'With views to the oceans, islands and mountains, glass was the obvious choice to capture the environment,' Myers says.

The house itself also shows industrial inspiration - a succession of four steel and concrete loft buildings set on three terraces that progress up the slope of the site and shadow the contours of the landscape. Each building has an exposed structural steel frame, with a metal deck framing and concrete retaining walls and floors. A garage and a guest house are set on the lower terrace, the main residence sits on the next, and there is an archive building on the upper level. 'The siting strategy was to make a series of smaller, discrete interventions,' explains Myers. 'This preserves and enhances the natural landscape.'

'Glass captures the environment'

Each pavilion is an open, loft space, enclosed by glazed garage-style doors, with an exposed structural frame and concrete floors.

The house is surrounded by xeriscaping to form a natural firebreak and this can be viewed through the expansive windows.

Right An 'elegant warehouse' in the tradition of Eames as well as Barton Myers' early houses, the Toro Canyon house remains open to its site, with spectacular canyon and ocean views.

Above The house is inspired by industrial buildings, and is essentially a series of four loft buildings set on three terraces on the canyonside.

Right Enormous glazed doors roll away into boxes on the ceiling to expose the house to its surroundings.

Toro Canyon's somewhat austere design is greatly softened by the ingenious use of enormous glazed aluminium sectional doors that roll away completely into boxes on the ceiling, throwing the building wide open to its surroundings. 'The sectional doors provide an amazing integration of indoors and outdoors,' says Myers. 'They're essentially curtain walls that move.'

Surprisingly, these 4.5-metre (15-feet) high by 5.5-metre (18-feet) wide glazed doors were not the most expensive glass element in the building – the house also has huge sliding doors which, at 3.7 metres (12 feet) high by 2 metres (6.5 feet) wide, were the largest size that could be guaranteed by the manufacturer as safe to slide. There are also clerestory windows that face north to the mountains while also welcoming in the soothing ocean breezes. To meet the tough energy codes of California, all the expanses of glass in Myers' house are double glazed and are also protected from the area's infamous indigenous fires by galvanized rolling insulated fire shutters, which form a second skin for this innovative canyon-side glass house.

Brazil: Rio de Janeiro Although Brazilian architect Oscar Niemeyer is lauded as a pioneer of the architectural use of reinforced concrete, this suburban home in Rio de Janeiro shows that he also had an innate understanding of the unique properties of glass as a material for building.

Constructed in 1985, three years before Niemeyer was awarded the Pritzker Architecture Prize, this family home in a Teresópolis neighbourhood is an example of the architect's light approach to modernist design. The geometric shape of the house is defined in Niemeyer's characteristic stark, white concrete, which greets the street with a closed, blank wall. However, the rear shows an altogether different and much more welcoming face, as full-height expanses of sparkling glass throw open the living areas to the sunshine and greenery of the private gardens. There, a serene L-shaped swimming pool mimics the bright outline of the building, and invites the light to bounce from the shining glass windows to the mirrored surface of the water and back again.

With minimal framing, the double-height glass panes draw light into both storeys of the house, but the interior is shielded from the strength of the sun by the wide-eaved roof, which juts out over the windows and emphasizes the angular quality of the design.

The interior is fashioned with Niemeyer's trademark sense of flow, which is evidenced in his famous public as well as very many private buildings. On the ground floor, a dining area, complete with green glass feature wall, leads directly into the lofty living area and its atrium, which channels more light and greenery into the centre of the home.

An artistically chiselled staircase sweeps towards the upper level and the luxuriously proportioned master bedroom, where a stunning sculptural window creates a handy nook – here put to use as an innovative indoor-outdoor smoking porch with views of the gardens below.

'A light approach to modernist design'

Above The neat L-shape of Niemeyer's house is mimicked in the shape of the swimming pool.

Left The glass theme continues inside the house, where an ornate glazed screen creates a dining enclave within the open-plan living space, which is punctuated by a narrow atrium filled with indigenous plants (right).

Above Inside, the house is an exercise in minimalism.

Right In his quest to create buildings that are light and transparent, Kogan's Casa Gama Issa is a 'white box' that opens completely to its surroundings thanks to full-height glass sliding doors.

Brazil: São Paulo 'The use of glass in the Casa Gama Issa is part of Marcio Kogan's endless search for light and transparency that can be see in all of his projects,' explains Renata Furlanetto, from the maverick Brazilian architect's São Paulo practice.

In fact, although his clients had not specified that their new home in Brazil's largest and most cosmopolitan city should be glazed in such dramatic fashion, they had discussed with Kogan their dreams of accommodating an enormous library in a living room with double-height ceilings and huge windows opening on to the garden. According to Kogan, they craved 'spaces of rare and

elegant proportions which relate to the exterior differently'.

The result, built in 2001, is a clean, white rectangle, completely glazed to the rear and overlooking a strip of mirror-flat swimming pool, 3 x 30 metres (10 x 100 feet), to reflect the geometry of the building. 'I think of a single enormous volume wrapping everything,' says Kogan. 'A white box.'

However, the box is easily opened. No less than two-thirds of the glass expanse that separates the living areas from the private gardens has the capacity to glide smoothly to the sides, revealing the room almost completely to its environment. The glass is

divided into six enormous panels, the central four of which are fitted with a system of floor pulleys and a mechanism in the ceiling, which allows them to retract effortlessly and precisely.

Their wish for a double-height living area granted, the owners have decorated the interior in stunning, minimalist white to create a bright and elegant indoor-outdoor space. Next door, in the kitchen and dining area, a vibrant orange worktop serves as an informal dining table, with chairs on just one side to face the huge plate-glass windows that reveal the unique São Paulo environment.

'Spaces of rare and elegant proportions'

Left As the glass panels roll effortlessly aside, the double-height living space is revealed to its setting.

Above and left The informal dining area, with its bright orange surface, is an ideal place to admire the gardens through the huge plate-glass windows.

UK: Petersham, London Glass houses are frequently designed to blend in with their surroundings, but in the case of this collection of homes built in 2002 in Petersham, south-west London, the intention was more to hide them from the outside world altogether and create a private environment of their own.

'This is an urban grouping of three courtyard houses, each looking into its own completely secluded garden,' explains architect Mike Stowell of Farrells, the practice behind the development. The arrangement is certainly introspective: the homes are surrounded on all sides by established trees, shrubs and high fences and, thanks to the bend in the 50-metre (164-feet) access lane, they are all but invisible from the nearest thoroughfare – exactly as the local planning authority had stipulated.

'An introspective development'

Above left Each of the glass homes at Petersham looks into its own private garden, and is completely invisible from the main road nearby.

Above right Louvres on the upper level allow the light to be manipulated.

Left The linear arrangement of rooms creates a gallery effect.

Left, below Thanks to glazed rooflights, the interior of the house is bright and airy.

Because the planners had emphasized the need to create a low-profile development, Farrells designed each home as a linear arrangement of rooms. Each has a dining room, kitchen, study and bedrooms, all accessed from a double-height gallery whose wall acts as the neighbouring home's boundary, to add to the seclusion. 'Glass is used extensively inside the houses, forming the gallery balustrades, the main stair wall and translucent glazing to the main bathrooms facing the gallery,' says Stowell. 'The main gallery space, which is the full length of each house, is top-lit with a glazed roof so the whole house is flooded with light, and this glazing, together with the full-height glazed walls, can be opened to provide cross-ventilation in the summer.'

Living space for each house is accommodated in stunning glazed pavilions, connected to the rest of the rooms by the gallery, and with full-height sliding doors to the gardens. The ingenious design of the site means that each pavilion is shielded from the public gaze by the remainder of the house, so the architects could afford to raise the height of the ceiling a little.

'The pavilions have full-height sliding glass walls to east and west,' says Stowell. 'In fact, all the major living spaces and bedrooms face south, and their glazed walls slide away to connect these rooms to their own private garden and create an indoor-outdoor living space.'

Above The main living area is contained in a glass pavilion with a high ceiling which was approved by the planners as it is not visible from the street.

US: Malibu, California 'In this house, the great glass façade gives the resident a sense of being among his surroundings, alive in the setting, not separated by the structural impediments of shelter,' says Stephen H. Kanner, the architect of the impressive Simpatico Sem, a glass cube-like residence that perches on the edge of a canyon in the hills of Malibu, California.

It was built in 2004 for a dentist client who had seen his former home – on the same site – razed to the ground in the fires that had ravaged Malibu a decade earlier. Fire resistance was therefore an important consideration in the design for the new house. This, coupled with the architect's desire to create a simple house that countered the rugged nature of the landscape all around, dictated the pared-down style.

Essentially, the house is a straightforward arrangement of two glass boxes, linked by a glazed staircase, with massive windows to bring in the spectacular surrounding views of the nearby mountains and the ocean in the distance. Forging a link with the landscape, as well as creating a necessary firebreak, are the xeriscaped gardens of irrigation-free indigenous plants that follow the perimeter of the house and are visible through the great glass windows.

'The glazing gives the best views down the canyon to the ocean,' says Kanner, 'and permits ample natural sunlight.' There was no need for tinting, as the glass is sheltered by the protruding structural elements, and the house's positioning makes the most of the sea breezes. In fact, the building is no more than 8 metres (26 feet) wide, and this lean profile means it has panoramic views of the canyon and the mountains, particularly from the master bedroom on the first floor.

At ground level, the kitchen and garage at the south end, and the living room and study to the north, have huge double-glazed openings that expose the view but are resilient to the ever-changing Californian weather. It is a house that observes nature, but remains steadfastly unconsumed by it.

'Alive in the setting'

Left Kanner's Simpatico Sem is essentially two glass boxes, linked by a glazed staircase, all on a narrow canyon-side site.

Right Only 25 feet wide, this four-bedroom home's west elevation has large dual-glazed windows with projections designed to shade the glass without tinting.

Left The double-height living space is glazed to give the best views of the canyon as well as the ocean.

Right A glass wall lights the stunning wood and steel open-tread staircase.

Above The large marble-clad bathrooms on the upper level are also substantially glazed.

Right A decked terrace leads from the master bedroom and allows the owner to step out into the setting.

UK: Hampstead, London 'Our idea was to create a building that could, to some extent, blur the inside-outside division,' says Shahriar Nasser of Belsize Architects, referring to the seven-bedroom home the practice designed in 2004 for a client and his large family in Hampstead, north London.

However, as the narrow building plot was right in the middle of the Heath Fringes Conservation Area, the local planners were more concerned that the new home would not create a division of architectural styles when placed next to its long-established neighbours. The solution was to use plenty of glass to create a sympathetic yet unobtrusively contemporary building that blends with its location, while also fulfilling the client's desire for a sociable, light-filled family home.

'We designed the cascading glass atrium to bring the light right into the heart of the building and also to create a central gathering area,' explains Nasser. The house is characterized by an unusual 'stepped' arrangement of tiered levels, which hug the central triple-height glass atrium. The living accommodation is provided in a series of rooms that are almost cell-like structures set in a U-shape around the atrium 'chapter'. The result is that, for such a large home, the areas for retreat, contemplation, rest and sleep are not in the least overwhelming and are instead small, comfortable and relaxing spaces. Light floods through the house from the atrium, which is made from structural double-glazed units fitted over steel sections with ladder beams in between, while the stunning steel and glass main staircase creates a sparkling centrepiece, formed from annealed glass in two laminated pieces.

All these features enhance the honest, open quality of this glass house. From the atrium entrance area, three layers of the building are visible above, while a huge sheet of structural glass set into the ground floor draws the eye to yet another level beneath the house, where the sparkling clarity of the glass is mimicked in the translucent quality of the basement pool.

Left From the front, this home in Hampstead, north London blends with its suburban setting.

Right A steel and glass staircase forms the centerpiece to the stunning three-storey atrium, whose technologically advanced glass means that the indoor temperature of the house is maintained, whatever the weather outside.

'Bringing light right into the heart of the building'

Left The spectacular glazed central section of the building creates a bright core of light and life in the home. The inside-outside theme is taken one step further as the glazed wall of the house opens completely so that in good weather the basement swimming pool can be accessed from both the house and the garden.

Above Windows to the side and the top of the pool mean the water becomes a feature of the interior of the house as well as the exterior.

New Zealand: Waitemata Harbour, Auckland This intriguing L-shaped house in a leafy suburb of Auckland was created as the ultimate party venue for a high-profile New Zealand family.

'Flow between the interior and the exterior was very important in the design of this home, because the owners were keen to use it for indoor-outdoor entertaining,' explains its architect, Daniel Marshall. 'It has certainly fulfilled its brief – the house has been used extensively for parties since it was built in 2001.'

Arranged courtyard-style, this substantial house is constructed mainly of stone-clad pre-cast concrete, which form two 'fins' either side of a glass-dominated entertaining and living space in the inside corner of the 'L'. This glass central section of the house can be opened up completely to the courtyard terrace and water feature, thanks to huge glass doors on ground floor, which vanish as they slide open, concealing themselves in specially designed wall cavities.

'For indoor-outdoor entertaining'

Left Full-height glass doors on the internal corner of the L-shaped house open completely to the courtyard and its swimming pool, which leads the eye beyond the boundary to the waters of Auckland's Waitemata Harbour.

Right On the suggestion of the owner, the main structure of the house is built from stone-clad pre-cast concrete and forms two 'fins', which house the private areas of the house, in contrast to the centre section, which is all sparkling glass and meant for public use.

'Sliding away the glass doors in the internal corner of the L-shape frees the inside edges of the house,' says Marshall. 'This is an important architectural device that links the diagonal flow of the building across the exterior terrace. The glass bisects the monolithic pre-cast structure of the house along the diagonal axis from the entry courtyard, through the main double-height living area.'

Not only does the sleek glass contrast with the rugged stone and concrete of the rest of the house, but it also zones the house into public and private spaces – bedrooms and bathrooms are contained in the concrete wings, while the centre of the home is welcoming to guests.

'The openness of the entry clearly defines the more public space in the house, and I wanted to recreate the allure of the hidden space behind the waterfall,' Marshall says. 'The glass makes a visual and metaphorical link, from the entrance to the terrace water feature, across the glass-tiled pool, and beyond towards the waters of Auckland's Waitemata Harbour.'

Left The view of the gardens through huge glass sliding doors is the only artwork in the neutrally decorated living space.

Above Natural materials in the bathrooms echo the setting.

Above right The simple white kitchen opens completely to the outdoor entertaining area.

'A towering observatory'

Left On the roof of the building is an impressive observatory – perhaps a sailor's lookout – glazed in glass blocks to complement the design of the remainder of the apartment block.

Right Full-height glazing creates an interior that is dominated by the river view.

UK: Hammersmith, London The fact that this London penthouse bears more than a passing resemblance to the deck of an ocean-going liner is no coincidence. Created by architect John Young of the Richard Rogers Partnership for himself in 1986, the apartment is actually named the Deck House – and Young's love of sailing clearly influences every aspect of the design.

Taking up the entire top floor of one of the three blocks that form the Thames Reach housing scheme right on the riverbank at Hammersmith, west London, the penthouse has a wonderful vantage point from which to absorb the riverscape, and Young has made the most of every opportunity to do so. The interior of the apartment is dominated by the water, which forms one wall of the double-height living area thanks to floor-to-ceiling gridded glass.

With its expansive teak floor, copious cabling and tubular steel supports, the apartment has all the hallmarks of a very well-crafted yacht. The sleeping platform, suspended in the living area and accessed by a stairway, makes the most of the river view and allows a good sailor to keep an eye on the weather and the water, day and night.

A kitchen and guests' quarters form the other half of the apartment, which is kept scrupulously shipshape thanks to the huge burnished-steel coffers that contain the everyday clutter that would not be welcome on board.

Upstairs is the apartment's 'deck' – the roof of the block – which is divided into two terraces, bounded by metal ship-style railings skirting the penthouse's most innovative feature: accessible from the interior, yet perched in its own free-standing structure on the roof, is the bathroom. A steel-framed construction of glass blocks with a clear glass roof, this is a bathroom like no other – it is more a towering observatory over the Thames, or perhaps a sailor's look-out.

Left The nautical theme continues inside with teak flooring, ship-style detailing and tubular steel supports.

Below The sleeping platform is suspended above the living space and accessed by an open-tread staircase.

Bottom The roof of the penthouse is inspired by the piers and bridges of the 19th century.

Following pages The glass block 'observatory' in the roof of the apartment building contains a stunning bathroom, minimally fitted in stainless steel.

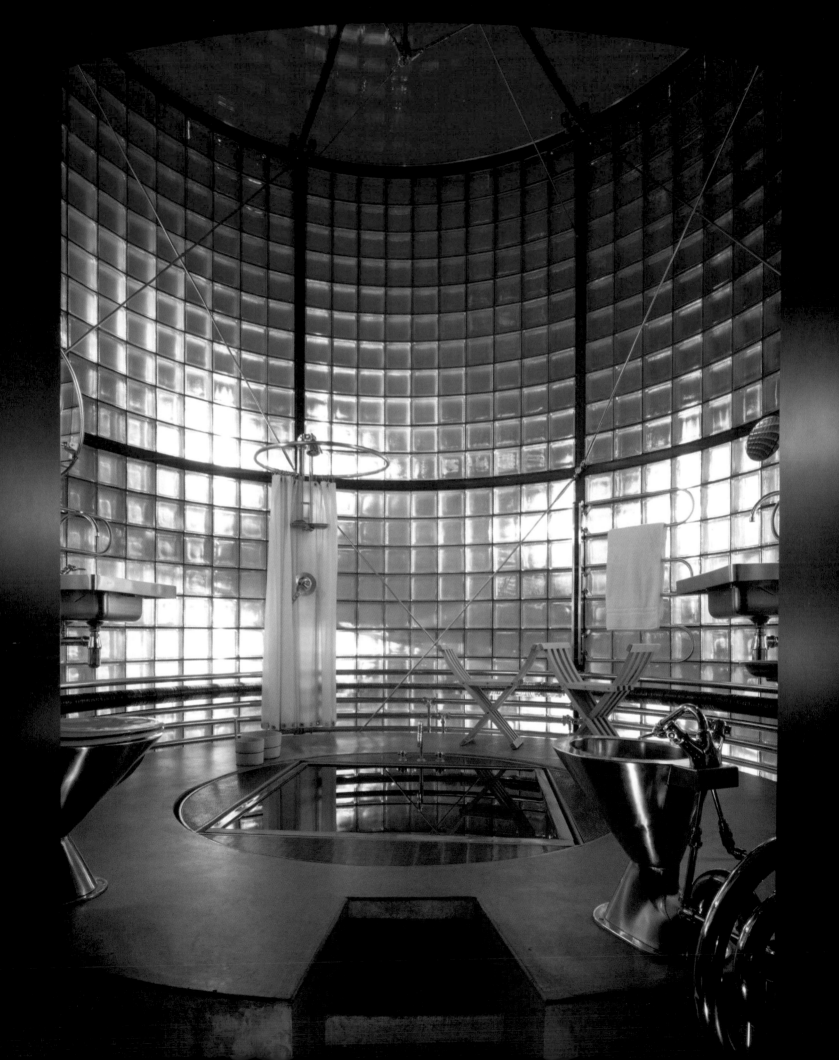

'A sculptural, modulated, Modernist box'

UK: Deal, Kent This boxy, rather industrial, rough render and glass house stands as something of a contrast to the string of conventional 1930s chalet bungalows that dot the Kent coast at Deal. Not only is this the only contemporary home for miles around, it is also designed upside-down.

'The brief, first and foremost, was to make the most of the stunning sea views and the sloping site,' explains architect Lynn Davis. 'The views are much better higher up, so the first major decision was to have the bedrooms on the lower ground floor and the living rooms on the upper ground floor.'

Taking advantage of the site's gradient, Lynn designed a home that would make life easy for the owners – Mauro Feltrin, of the Italian dynasty behind the contemporary furniture design company Arper, and his wife Jo Radcliffe, who runs the Deal-based arm of the business with him.

Although the house is very tall, the layout is incredibly user-friendly, with two entrance doors at ground level – one into a 'mud' room and the other into a hall with access to the gently pitched staircase, which radiates in short flights around a central light-well. The flight downstairs leads to the house's four bedrooms and the family bathroom, while climbing upwards reveals first a utility room and private terrace, and then another short flight of stairs opens into the stunning living space that dominates the upper floor. A huge, double-height split-level glazed box, the family's open-plan living accommodation is dominated by 180-degree panoramic views of the sea through full-height glazed windows and doors. While the kitchen and bathroom are set on the higher level, the lower level of the space leads out through enormous glass doors on to generous Iroko-decked balconies, bounded on one side by glass blocks to provide shelter from the sea breezes while maintaining contact with the view.

'The clients wanted a clean, sculptural, modulated, modernist box,' says Davis. 'The constraints of the site dominated the main form, but the play of the double-height cubes on the south of the site and the rhythm of the elements wrapping around the staircase gives the house a more articulated external presence.'

Above The front entrance, which leads to the light-filled staircase.

Left Views to the sea characterise the split-level living space. Many of the materials for the house, including the oak floors, were chosen in Italy and brought over, and the plain buffed interior plaster inside matches the rough render of the exterior walls.

Below, left and right At ground level, the bathrooms and bedrooms see the cliffs from a different perspective. The cream bathroom tiles were imported from Italy, while the rooflight was inserted so that the owners could lie in the bath and look at the stars. The simple bedrooms are left plain and unadorned in line with the owners' wish for a home with an industrial feel.

Right The upper level dining area has a bird's eye view of the sea.

Canada: Toronto From the front, this appears to be a conventional family home on a quiet street in suburban Toronto, complete with typical blank white walls and pitched roofs. However, behind this unassuming façade, the main part of the house is set right in the middle of an area of real Canadian wilderness, a thickly forested ravine that monopolizes the back of this long plot.

That is not the only surprise, though. In fact, this is not so much one house as a series of little homes, clustered together to form a progression of areas that stretch from the suburban context of the front to the natural setting at the back.

'As the house progresses, it gradually opens up to the wilderness,' explains architect Seth Stein, who in 2000 designed the home as two white interconnecting cubes, distanced from the house by no fewer than three courtyards.

Inside the two cubes are four mini-houses that form the family's innovative bedroom accommodation. Linking the cubes is a stunning, double-height living space, constructed of luminous sand-blasted glass.

'This house was conceived as a receptacle for light,' says Stein. 'The enclosure is of translucent glass, so it has the effect of transmitting light throughout the house. At night it lights up like a lantern.'

One of the most ingenious aspects of this design is that the light in the living section can be manipulated thanks to a system of aluminium louvres under the glass roof. These can be electronically controlled, and as they overhang the building by 5 metres (16 feet) in the direction of the ravine they have a dramatic effect on the internal climate.

'The louvres also act as a canopy,' says Stein. 'They reach out towards the forest and connect the inside to the outside. They diminish the boundary so much that, when you are in the living room, you feel as if you could easily be sitting in the forest.'

'Opens up to the wilderness'

Right Backing a ravine, this suburban Canadian home is a series of glass boxes.

Left Full-height glazing in the living area is sheltered by a system of louvres which can be manipulated to provide shade.

Left The stark living space is dominated by the natural wilderness outside the enormous windows.

Right The simple geometry of the building is replicated inside, with a solid rectangular staircase and oblong pillars.

US: Bel Air, California 'The use of so much glass in the design of this building was not only to create transparency and light,' explains architect Zoltan E. Pali of SPF:a. 'Here, glass is a key component.'

A designer himself, Pali's client had a particular desire for a white house, with an indoor-outdoor connection and minimalist beauty, to be constructed for him on a narrow strip of land on the edge of a steep canyon in Bel Air, California. However, the auspices were not good. Early soil testing revealed that the site was not at all suited to residential development unless the structure could be rooted to the forty-five-degree canyon-side with concrete friction piles, dug 27 metres (89 feet) below the surface. Meanwhile, the local planning guidelines for the hillside meant that the design options were strictly limited.

Top The façade of the home is designed to meet the client's desire for minimal beauty, with white render broken by large swathes of full-height white-framed glass panes.

Left and right The two halves of the home are linked by a sparkling glass bridge, with views to the canyon on both sides.

'Glass is a key component'

Left Openable windows in the sleek living area welcome in the atmosphere of the landscape as well as the view.

Right The direct sunlight is screened by a series of limestone louvres on the staircase that leads down from the bridge to the kitchen and dining areas.

Undaunted by this conundrum, in 2004 Pali created a home that is not a burden either to the site or to the surrounding landscape. To reduce the weight of the building on the local geology, the ground-floor living space takes the form of a large courtyard, while floor-to-ceiling panes of glass – narrow on the first floor, and wide on the ground – ensure that the design of the house does not encroach on the setting. In fact, it welcomes it in.

At the same time, though, glass is put to work as a way of connecting the house to itself. Designed in two distinct halves, the building is linked by a sparkling glass box bridge that gives views not just of the outside but of the inside, too. Crossing from the private accommodation of the western block, it is possible to see through the transparent tunnel and into the free-flow public areas of the house on the south-eastern side. In their turn, the ground-floor kitchen, dining and sitting room flow one into the next, and are dominated by floor-to-ceiling windows with wide canyon views. Above them, the master suite and private terrace have a façade of narrow white-framed glass panes that allow the vista to seep into every corner.

'As you move through the circulation spaces you will catch a glimpse of a moment,' says Pali, 'and that moment is welcomed in by the glass.'

'Modern, with a vernacular touch'

Ibiza, Spain 'The white of the glass has a relevance to the architecture of the island - it's modern with a vernacular touch,' says Tibor Martin of Spanish architectural practice Vincens + Ramos, which created this highly unusual glass house on the island of Ibiza in 2004.

In fact, although the house is built entirely of glass, it is completely obscured and is used simply as a cladding. 'The white glass just takes the place of brick or stone,' explains Martin, 'but it is very useful functionally. The glass is very easy to clean with a pressure washer, which is important as sandstorms are common on the island. It also has excellent thermal properties, as there is a cavity between the glass and the brick behind, which creates a vacuum that keeps the house cool in hot weather.'

Originally, though, it was planned as a much more conventional building. 'The client bought the property when the structure was already in place,' says Martin. 'It is so difficult to obtain planning

Left The white glass cladding on this unusual home on the island of Ibiza references the local vernacular architecture, but is highly practical as it can be cleaned easily.

Below The house is surrounded by the natural landscape of the Balearics.

Following pages Surrounded by sun deck, the white glass house has spectacular views of the Mediterranean and out to Formentera

permission on Ibiza, so we had to work with it. The glass cladding was a way of reflecting the local architecture, but in a more contemporary way.'

The house's accommodation is arranged over three floors. On the ground floor are reception rooms, as well as three bedrooms for the owner's children and one for the maid, while the top floor has the master suite, with its own gym, solarium and two bathrooms.

There is also a semi-basement floor that leads out to its own terrace and has a guest room of the same proportions as the master bedrooms, the children's playroom and a self-contained annexe.

With such an expansive interior it would be a shame not to be able to see out and, by way of a contrast to the obscured glass, there are plenty of clear glass windows too, which give glorious views of Formentera and the Mediterranean.

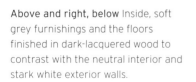

Above and right, below Inside, soft grey furnishings and the floors finished in dark-lacquered wood to contrast with the neutral interior and stark white exterior walls.

Right, above On the top floor, the bathroom is fitted in simple white sanitary ware, continuing the monochromatic theme.

95

With plenty of glass used in its conversion, this former Victorian stable block in London is now a striking, light-filled contemporary home.

3 Breathing New Life

Glass is a great rejuvenator of buildings, bringing light and life to spaces that have become dowdy or dull. Whether a glazed extension or a substantial refurbishment, glass brings new purpose and inspiration to tired buildings and, in some cases, a whole new character.

One of the earliest and most influential of conversions using glass is the celebrated Maison de Verre in Paris, the result of a collaboration in 1931 between furniture and interior designer Pierre Chareau, architect Bernard Bijvoet and metal worker Louis Dalbet. Commissioned to create an impressive home and consulting room for a well-to-do Parisian doctor, the trio's job was made all the more complicated by the refusal of an elderly tenant to vacate the top floor of the building. Chareau was charged with redesigning the house in a contemporary style but without completely rebuilding it, and the project therefore became a conversion.

Ingeniously Chareau scooped out the lower floors of the building and replaced the walls with industrial style glass panes, translucent glass block and bare steel, transforming the building beyond all recognition by capitalizing on glass's greatest gift – to bring light and a new lease of life. A stunning glass house in its own right, the Maison de Verre positively glows as darkness falls in the city, and is recognised as a great architectural landmark.

Since then, glass has proved itself to be the ideal material for reinvention. From the point of view of design, it can be used creatively to add originality to standard homes, to complement an existing building, or to create a striking point of contrast. Practically, modern glass is easy to work with, quick to install and now has good thermal properties.

Above all, adding glass to a dismal and neglected house – whether in the shape of enormous window panes or doors, or clever glazed roofs, or even transparent interior walls – immediately gives that building a new identity and a second chance to become a light-filled, contemporary living space, flooded with natural energy and a sense of warmth and well-being.

This wonderful array of qualities makes glass an invaluable resource for architects who work with listed and other old and characterful buildings. When used with a light touch, glass can effect subtle changes that update and improve a period home, while taking nothing away from its traditional charm. In fact, it is hard to spot glass conversions to the vast majority of period homes, so delicate is the change that there is no visible sign from the front at all, with much of the new design with glass only in evidence from the back. In this way, though, the original house is brought into the modern day in a respectful manner, and with good design, even a contemporary glass conversion need not compromise the integrity of the traditional architecture.

However, the main aim of the glass conversion is more often than not to allow for a modern style of living in an old house and this is where glass really comes into its own. The reanimated buildings that feature on the following pages are a true tribute to the great capacity of glass to transform, enrich and enliven much-loved existing homes.

UK: Chelsea, London Lord Rogers has made no secret of the fact that he is greatly inspired by the work of glass-house pioneer Pierre Chareau, and there are several apparent references to the Maison de Verre in the design of many of Rogers's commercial projects. Notable among these, of course, is the Lloyds of London building, with its acres of opaque glass.

However, Chareau's influence does not stop there, and Rogers's desire for buildings that are structurally clear and unadorned extends to his work in residential architecture, including his own home – a sedate Victorian building facing Christopher Wren's Royal Hospital in Chelsea.

Lord and Lady Rogers's home is actually two terraced houses that were knocked together in 1987, although there is very little sign of this from the outside. Inside, however, the house has

Below The house is formed from two terraced homes knocked into one, with the interior scooped out to create a bright, airy space.

Right The piazza-style main living area, on the first floor, is dominated by the light and views from eight large, south-facing sash windows.

'Structurally clear and unadorned'

undergone the same 'scooping-out' procedure similar to that of the Maison de Verre. The main living area, on the first floor, is now an impressive double-height space, flooded with light from eight south-facing sash windows, which frame the view of the Royal Hospital and its well-kept grounds.

As Lady Rogers is a professional chef and co-owner of London's River Café, it is perhaps no surprise that the kitchen is the focal point of the piazza-style living space, and is equipped with industrial stainless-steel fittings.

Outside, a glass extension stands in the space once occupied by a small courtyard and creates a shell for a beautiful stainless-steel staircase. This feature, designed by Laurie Abbott, connects the unassuming street-level entrance to the expansive first-floor living area and then continues up to the bedrooms and bathrooms on the top floor.

This conversion reflects Rogers's desire to live en famille. The ground floor is set aside as an apartment for his mother-in-law, while the easy flow of the living area effortlessly accommodates family gatherings and parties, and provides a gallery-style exhibition space for his collection of modern art. In this house, it is clear to see many of the underlying principles of Rogers's – and to an extent Chareau's – commitment to modern architecture.

Above A stainless steel staircase, designed by Laurie Abbott, connects the three storeys of the house.

Above Interior doors pivot to allow the interior to flow uninterrupted.

Right The sleek kitchen is the hub of the home.

UK: Camden, London This London home has something of a split personality. From the street it has all the decorum of the classic Georgian doll's house – its white frontage has a smart black door and typical large sash windows – but, climb the black-and-white tiled steps and walk inside, and a completely different house is revealed.

Instead of the expected 1800s layout is a bright and expansive interior, high-ceilinged, spacious and flooded with light thanks to a huge glass extension that consumes the back of the house and opens on to the garden by virtue of the large, pivoting glazed doors.

This is the home of architect Steve Marshall, of Munkenbeck+ Marshall, and his wife, who bought the house in 2000. Extensions and ill-conceived add-ons had made a jumble of the original design, and the house was a warren of tiny spaces that had been used as consulting rooms by the doctors who had previously owned the house. The Marshalls set about stripping it back to its original 19th-century shell.

The house's dramatic reincarnation was achieved by extending the building 1 metre (3 feet) into the garden, where the ground was levelled to give a smooth transition between inside and out.

'Thrown open to the outside space'

Left and below A series of dramatic 4-metre high glass doors swivel to open the ground floor living space entirely to the garden.

Above By sinking the floor, a greater ceiling height was achieved in the new glazed living area.

Right The open staircase is in keeping with the fluid living space.

Above Dramatic windows in the first-floor bedrooms create a garden backdrop.

Similarly, a section of the floor was removed to increase the volume of the inside space – the fireplace that remains gives a hint to its original level – giving a luxurious ceiling height of 4 metres (13 feet).

The extension now forms the rear part of the house, an open-plan and fluid space that incorporates the Marshalls' living and dining areas as well as an ingenious sunken kitchen. With a completely glazed rear wall, light floods into the house, and by swivelling the series of four impressive 4-metre (13-foot) high glass doors through ninety degrees, the house is thrown completely open to the outside space.

Above the living area, the main bedroom is accommodated in its own box-like glass enclosure, with dramatic windows giving views over the smart, contemporary courtyard garden that forms an extra, outdoor living space for this unconventional, rejuvenated period home.

UK: Stockwell, London This Grade II-listed Victorian house in Stockwell, south London was in a sorry state when it was bought by a couple with two young children in 1998. Having been occupied by squatters for several years, the house had been stripped of its original features, charred by fire, and left leaking and rotting.

Its refurbishment then was something of a challenge, and following a limited architectural competition, London-based David Mikhail Architects were brought in to transform the building into a light and spacious home suitable for the young family.

The appalling condition of the house meant that obtaining planning permission to refurbish it was not as difficult as the Grade II listing usually implies and, thanks to sympathetic neighbours and the support of English Heritage, a scheme to restructure the inside was approved, with work beginning on-site in 1999.

The brief was to improve the relationship between the house and the garden, and Mikhail achieved this by removing the floor at street level and to rebuild it a full metre lower, at the level of the garden. This created a new one-and-a-half-storey family room,

Left This Victorian house has been updated by the insertion of a one-and-a-half-storey family room, complete with full-height glazing to the rear.

Right The living area is set on varying levels to designate areas of use.

'Transformed into a light and spacious family home'

terraced to provide designated areas, and dominated by a spectacular full-height sliding glass panel, which opens to reveal the garden.

'The glass is toughened and double glazed, in three panels 4.5 metres high,' explains Mikhail, 'and was structural silicone glazed into the cedar sliding door frame. This means the glass is completely flush with the timber door frame, so no beads. It was brought in by hand, so was much more affordable than one big panel.'

The building's most notable new characteristic though is the glass staircase, top-lit by a new glass roof and traced by a series of windows that at night form a spectacular illuminated column, that runs from the top to the bottom of the house.

Left The full-height glazed panel slides away to reveal the house to the garden.

Right The spectacular glass staircase is lit from above by a carefully positioned rooflight.

Below Thanks to the extensive glazing, the family living space is bright and airy.

UK: Highgate, London London-based architect Eva Jiricna is well known for her sculptural glass designs, which grace impressive homes as well as high-profile commercial buildings. Her design for a stunning glass and steel staircase for a London branch of Joseph caused a stir in 1988, and she has gone on to experiment with the ornamental properties of glass for both interior design and architectural use.

One of her most striking projects to date is this re-imagining of a house in Highgate, north London. It was designed and built in 1957 by Ove Arup in conjunction with the Rhodesian architect Erhard Lorenz, but by 1991 the building had become a little careworn and was put on the market. It was immediately snapped up by a young South African who had grown up in California, and his wife, a New Yorker, who recognized the house's potential and determined to lavish some much-needed attention on it.

Below The house was designed by Ove Arup in the 1950s, but updated in 1991 by glass expert Eva Jiricna.

Right The new pavilion addition, formed of a series of linked, skim pin jointed columns supporting a diaphragm roof tied down at the front and back, wraps around the end of the pool and opens up to the south.

'The glazed structure has become such an intrinsic part of its architecture'

Below The lap pool sits parallel to the house as a formal element in the composition, separating the lawn from the sloping, more wild section of the garden.

Bottom Enclosure and privacy are provided by a variety of glazed screens.

Above Double glazed structural glass walls enclose the new space, divided into areas for living, dining and exercising.

To this end, the couple brought in Jiricna, who was charged with the task of modernizing and extending the house to suit the 'West Coast' lifestyle of its new owners without compromising the essential architectural qualities of the building and its setting. Most pressing was the need to open up the ground floor and add a glass conservatory extension – which would be used as a living and dining area – and to wrap around the new lap pool, which was a main requirement.

This glass addition has resulted in a house filled with light and life. It takes the form of a series of pavilions, created from double-glazed structural glass walls. Glazed screens help divide the space and provide some privacy, while grey stone flooring, inside and out, helps to unify the interior and exterior spaces.

Jiricna's trademark glass touches can be found all over the house, and tie in with the glazed structure that has become such an intrinsic part of its architecture. The refitted kitchen has doors of translucent glass, while upstairs the master bedroom has been opened up to include a new balcony with glass balustrades that accentuate the open views across the garden and link to the theme of the pavilion below.

US: Hollywood Hills, California This landmark house, high in the Hollywood Hills, was designed by John Lautner in the 1960s and was purchased two decades later by entrepreneur Jim Goldstein, who invited the architect to come back and refurbish it to his own taste.

Clinging to a slope overlooking the ocean, the house was originally conceived as a wedge shape, with bedrooms and a kitchen-diner leading into a living room that would open wide beneath a striking angular canopy. As the first owners had a dream of camping 'under the stars' in their home, Lautner had set 750 water glasses into the grid of the concrete vault to allow the interior to be dappled with light. Ingeniously, this part of the house was completely open to the exterior, separated from the pool terrace outside by only a curtain of forced air.

Left Like the lair of a James Bond villain, this house is tucked away 400 feet up into the Hollywood Hills, with superb views all around.

Below Glass walls allow the vista to unfold as the house progresses on this extraordinary site.

'Unframed walls of glass expose the room to the landscape'

However, the openness of the living space proved impractical for Goldstein, and when Lautner returned, along with fellow architect Helene Arahuete, the pair sealed off the opening with enormous unframed glass windows, to protect the house from the elements without interrupting the view. 'The glass was added to suit the site,' says Arahuete, 'as well as the best views and the spatial continuity.'

The renovation work evolved over a period of many years, and when Lautner died in 1994, Arahuete continued the process in a sympathetic vein. The house's steel mullions, which fouled the view, were replaced with sheets of tempered glass, while the skylights were enlarged and fitted with electronic systems so that they could be opened and adjusted easily to bring light and air into the living areas.

The master suite is set into the hillside, with porthole windows into the swimming pool on one side and the other sides formed by unframed walls of glass that roll back to expose the room to the landscape.

Right Unframed glass walls connect the extraordinary living space to the panoramic view.

Below The angular canopy conceals the glass-sided house, clinging to the mountaintop.

Full-height frameless glass doors
fold back to open the interior to the
exterior space.

Above Floor-to-ceiling windows allow the master bedroom to jut out into its surroundings.

Left The natural vegetation is reflected in the glass sides of the house.

UK: Kensington, London This urban plot in west London had already been put to a number of uses when architect Seth Stein set about redeveloping it in 1995. 'Although the site was derelict when we took it on, we were keen to work with the existing historic fabric and expand on it,' explains Stein. 'In 1880 it was built as stables, and fifteen years later it became a builder's yard, and then a factory block was added. I wanted to extend the sequence, from the brick of the Victorian era, up to the concrete, steel and glass of 120 years later.'

The best way to do this, he decided, was to create a courtyard by refurbishing the standing building, and adding a 12-metre (40-foot) glazed gallery to form an L-shape. 'Courtyards allow you to achieve a greater contact with the outside space, while maintaining privacy,' says Stein. 'It's really a much better alternative to the typical London back garden, where security can be an issue and only one portion of the house has the benefit of looking to the outside. But in the courtyard design, much more of the house is overlooking an external space and there is scope for glazing to create even greater openness.'

'From the brick of the Victorian era, to the concrete, steel and glass of 120 years later'

Left A spectacular 12-metre glazed gallery encloses the courtyard garden of this former 19th-century stable block.

Conversion of the stable block to create family living accommodation allowed Stein to glaze the rear wall and install a spectacular orange-framed glass panel, made from a piece of Pilkington glass strong enough to walk on. This glazing brings light from the courtyard flooding into the main living areas of the home, while glass on the upper storey lights the bedrooms. Meanwhile, the gallery has very little structure at all, and is formed from a series of frameless glass panels to create a long, light-flooded walkway.

'The L-shape allows an exploration of the transition from the external to the enclosed space, public to private,' says Stein. 'The glass lets the occupants have a much better view of the outside and to absorb more natural light, and this in turn has a great influence on their moods.'

Above The house's rectangular form is contrasted with circular rooftop protrusions.

Above Angled interior walls define the living space without the need for doors.

Right The orange-framed glass panel in the living area gives onto the courtyard and allows light to flood the home.

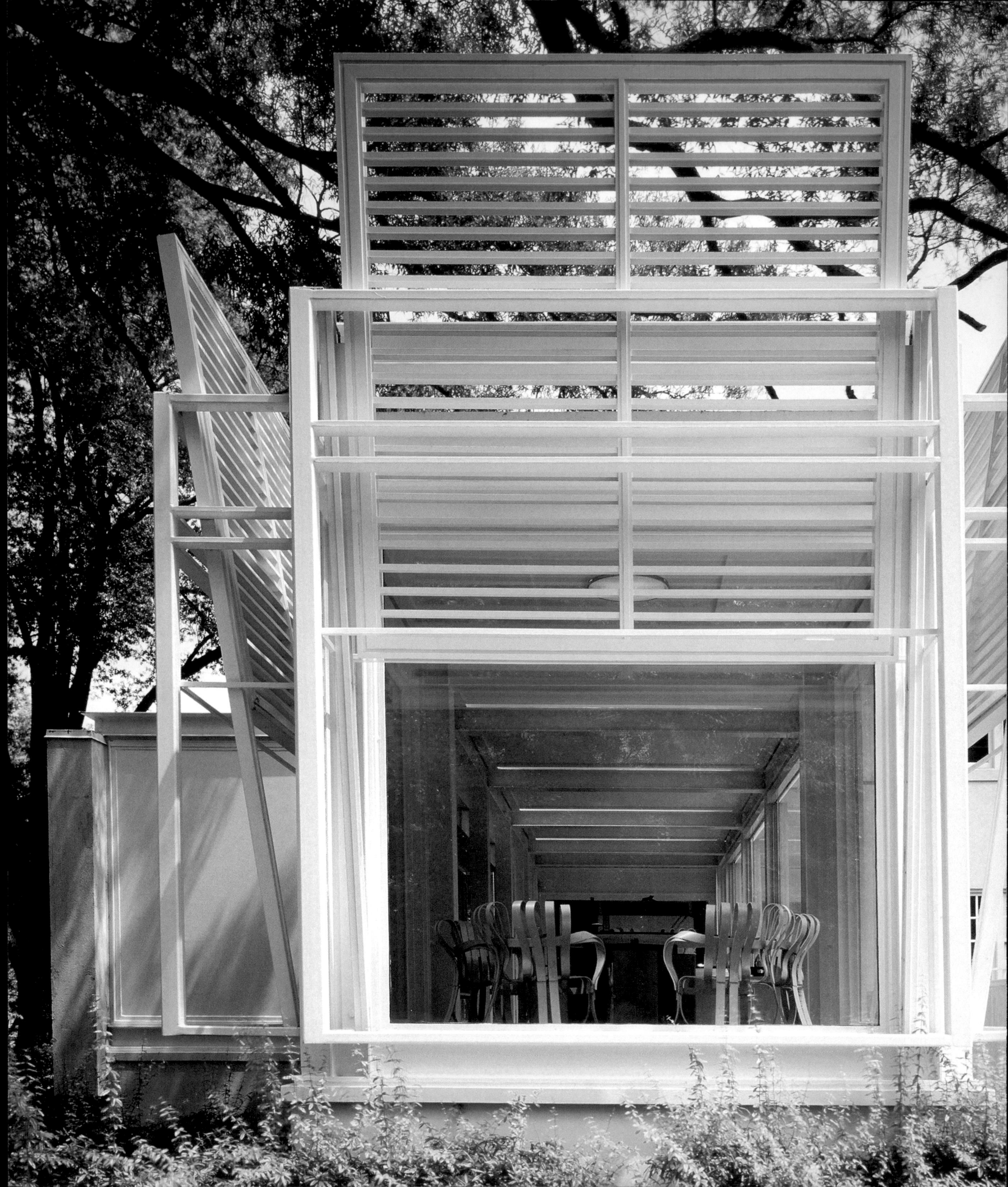

US: Charlotte, North Carolina 'The passage of time and the subdivision of the original property had caused severe damage to the house and almost total destruction to the formal gardens,' explains architect Kenneth E. Hobgood, who was brought in to renovate this historic 1914-built house in the Meyers Park, one of the longest-established neighbourhoods in Charlotte, North Carolina.

Although Hobgood restored the main part of the house to its original condition – retaining the arrangement of rooms around the central staircase – the most striking feature of the refurbishment work is the new rear extension, with its three sides of glass, that now juts out into the Italianate gardens. 'There was originally a garden pavilion on the site,' says Hobgood, 'but this addition accommodates the kitchen and breakfast room as well as a garden room. To provide privacy and sun control, 3-metre by 3-metre mechanical shutters move vertically on metal tracks.'

Left The new metal and glass extension sits comfortably between the house, its garage and its garden. The distinctive shutters can be adjusted mechanically to offer shade and privacy.

Below Jutting out into the Italianate gardens, the glass addition links this established home to its setting.

'Bringing the house up-to-date while preserving its style'

Left The long, narrow kitchen echoes the rectangular design of the glass extension.

Below The central hall, with its stunning steel and slate staircase, remains at the core of the home.

Right Contemporary glass-topped tables mirror the expanses of rectangular glazing and give this home a modern edge.

The new metal-framed extension is something of a departure from the original architecture of the main part of the house, but as it fits in neatly between the building, the garage and the garden, it gives the exterior of the property a completeness that it previously lacked. Bridging old and new on the inside is the refurbished central hall, now redesigned as a large cubic volume constructed of plain sawn maple around a new steel and slate staircase. This central space connects to all the original rooms of the house and, thanks to its contemporary style, serves as a preview to the generously proportioned new addition.

With its frame painted white to match the render of the exterior of the main house, and with a superb view over the carefully tended gardens, the glass box extension creates a fluid and airy space in this traditional home, bringing it up to date while also preserving the principal elements of its original style.

This Brazilian tree house home by
Marcio Kogan melds convincingly with
its forested surroundings, thanks to its
unframed walls of glass.

4 At Home in the Landscape

In a world filled with so much natural beauty, it is no surprise that many people want not just to see it, but to live in it. Glass provides the ideal building material for houses that are as much in the landscape as they are of it.

'Organic buildings are the strength and lightness of the spiders' spinning, buildings qualified by light, bred by native character to environment, married to the ground,' Frank Lloyd Wright is quoted as saying, and there is no material better suited to the attainment of these goals than sparkling, translucent glass.

Wright also commented, 'Buildings, too, are children of Earth and Sun,' and it is clear from the examples of spectacularly sited glass houses in this chapter, that architects who know their craft and have the skill to capitalize on the great properties of glass, are able to create homes that are as much a part of their environment as they are functional shelters.

Although the 'organic' style of architecture espoused by Wright and his fellow early American modernists calls for a prioritizing of the direct aesthetic link between inside and outside, many of the architects who followed were able to evolve this concept into a dialogue between the building and its environment.

While many more contemporary exponents of glass in architecture take their inspiration directly from the surrounding landscape when imagining a new place to live, there are also those who like to indulge in a little interplay between the setting and the conceived structure.

Some glass houses, such as those of Marcio Kogan, Lord Foster and Zoltan E. Pali, illustrated on the following pages, are built in and around the existing natural forms, but do not try to replicate them. Others take delight in challenging the local environment with the unnatural precision of their design and the obviously manufactured quality of their building materials.

However, the imposition of expanses of clear or translucent glass in place of more substantial materials gives these buildings an air of insubstantiality that would not otherwise have been achieved. In this way it is possible to create a building that is almost a deception of nature. Despite the obvious unnaturalness of its design and construction, the building treads so lightly on the landscape that it is able to harness the awe-inspiring beauty of its natural surroundings, and by pulling them in, consumes its very environment for the enrichment of itself.

Brazil: Rio de Janeiro This elongated stone and glass box, by São Paulo-based architect Marcio Kogan, is so much in and of its surroundings that vast ancient ferns poke through to the interior at roof level. Essentially a glass-sided tree house, it is set high in the canopy of the Brazilian Atlantic rainforest, where it takes to extremes the concept of bringing the outside in.

Although Kogan is best known for the urban, box-like designs that punctuate the skyline of São Paulo, for this project he embraced the lush natural landscape of this undeveloped swathe of mountains and forest north of Rio de Janeiro. He devised a scheme based on minimalist, geometric principles, but inset with glass to give every room a vista of the lush vegetation all around.

Kogan's task was hampered by the fact that he took over the project when work had already begun. The clients, a wealthy couple from Rio who dreamed of having a rainforest retreat, had fired their first architect, but not before the skeleton of the house had been embedded into the landscape. In addition, a heavy steel entrance bridge had been constructed over the creek that cuts through the secluded, 0.6-hectare (1.5-acre) property. With little option but to incorporate these elements, Kogan set about

Left Kogan's glass-sided tree house is enveloped by the natural vegetation of the dense Brazilian rainforest.

Right The house all but disappears as the trees are reflected in the great expanses of shining glass.

'Appears to float among the treetops'

Above The pool room, with its narrow strip of water, is set with local stone to blend with the landscape visible through the glass wall.

imposing his own order. Dissatisfied with the apparent lack of perfect symmetry in the basic structure, he cantilevered the first floor and ceiling slabs beyond the stilts, thereby diminishing their visual impact and creating the paradoxical illusion of an elongated stone box that appears to have no weight at all.

The accommodation of four suites on the first floor – a guest bathroom, a kitchen and the living and dining rooms – appears simply to float among the treetops. At ground level, a heated pool and dry sauna are embedded into the natural stone and dominated completely by the leafy wilderness that abounds just the other side of the enormous, fixed-glass window.

Above Glazed on all sides, the sleek living room is on a level with the treetops.

Left Wooden shutters provide privacy in the bedroom and also shield the interior from the sun.

Left The villa's rooftop pool, protected by sliding glass walls, has a bird's eye view of the Mediterranean.

Below and following pages Two tubes of steel arc from the rear of the new pool, over the house and down to the new lower bedroom level, supporting a net of steel cords, over which vines are to be trained to create a 'green veil' over the building.

France: Saint-Jean-Cap-Ferrat This prestigious resort in the south of France is no stranger to the work of internationally renowned architects – Le Corbusier, Eileen Gray and Oscar Niemeyer have all designed villas here – and one more famous name was added in 1999 when Lord Foster undertook to update the 1950s-built Villa Messidor.

This striking white and glass edifice clings to the mountain overlooking the Mediterranean and is arranged in three stepped storeys that climb down towards the water. However, the building was very different when Lord Foster first came across it.

In common with its illustrious neighbours, the villa was originally designed on Modernist principles fused with the local commitment to create buildings that are at home in the landscape. Alterations made over the next five decades though had compromised the villa's relationship with its setting, and cluttered its Modernist style. Neglect of the boundaries, and the addition of

'Enhancing the rugged vernacular'

an artificial rock garden filled with non-indigenous plants had also taken the house further from its original concept.

Lord Foster set about restoring the integrity of the villa by developing further the rugged vernacular of the original architecture. In doing so, he elected to remove a whole floor of the building to create a huge double-height living space, facing the sea.

The natural next stage was to bring together the six large windows that already existed into one enormous wall of glass on the sea-facing side to give spectacular panoramic views of the Med. The quirk in the design of this however is that Foster has positioned the glass wall at an angle to the building, so that on each level the wall slopes out from the ceiling to the floor level to create a fabulous vantage point and to increase the feeling of being at one with the setting. This is further enhanced when the glass slides aside, revealing the interior of the house entirely to the seascape and the mountainside setting.

Left Glass doors on the bedroom level provide a superb vantage point.

Below left The elegant white and glass villa steps down towards the sea, and is characterised by the two arcs of stainless steel tubing designed to support vines as well as a sail to provide shelter from the intense heat of the south of France.

Right The glazed wall of the double-height living space opens entirely to give an uninterrupted view of the sea.

Belgium: West Flanders With the brief to design a family house on what was once the vegetable patch of a country mansion in West Flanders, Belgian architect Stéphane Beel found that the only constraint on the design was that there were no constraints. 'The absence of restriction emerged to be the only limitation,' he explains. 'It led to the intention to do "almost nothing", an elementary gesture that, in all its simplicity, doesn't interfere but consolidates.'

With the vegetable garden already divided into walled sections, Beel designed the house as a long, narrow envelope of a building, as, he says, 'a new wall to live in'. Its sequence of rooms, reached one through the other, are arranged in linear fashion, with bedrooms at either extremity and a glazed living section in the centre. The entrance is also in the middle, but this quickly gives way to the bright box of the living area to one side, and the kitchen and dining area to the other. Both sections of the house have full-height glazing, part of which opens to the outside. The surroundings are further brought into the interior thanks to a glazed atrium that eats into the living space and brings with it light and a sense of the outdoors. 'Garden and orchard become interior in the glazed central zone,' explains Beel. 'The inside volumes are like big pieces of furniture that grade privacy and can be open or closed, inside and outside.'

Even in the parts of the house that are not fully glazed, there are huge windows that help to connect the house to its environment. 'In strategic places the closed walls are cut away and opened, to frame the landscape and to give it dimension,' says Beel. 'By hiding and showing, these openings yield something of the rooms and the gardens behind. The relationship between the house and its environment is an alliance.'

Designed as 'a new wall to live in', this Belgian house is a linear succession of rooms. At its centre is a striking glazed living space, whose full-height glass doors slide aside to unite the inside with the outside.

'An alliance between the house and its environment'

Left The natural materials of the interior chime with the garden setting.

Below Even in areas of the home not dominated by the great glass doors, smaller windows, such as these in the kitchen, provide a constant view of the surrounding.

New Zealand: Great Barrier Island 'The Great Barrier Island House was designed as a family retreat for holidaying,' explains architect Tim Hay of Fearon Hay, based in Auckland, New Zealand. 'Really it's an escape from the mainland.'

This house, which was completed in 2005, certainly puts some distance between itself and the nearest civilization. To get to it necessitates a 90-kilometre (56-mile) boat or plane journey north-east of Auckland to Great Barrier Island – known locally as Aotea – then, assuming the tide is low enough, a trip in a four-wheel-drive vehicle across sand dunes and an estuary. It is no surprise that only 900 people live permanently on the island's 285 square kilometres (110 square miles). The land is virtually untouched by human habitation and remains naturally rugged and a little hostile. Even the owners of the house designed by Fearon Hay found their ideal 6.5-hectare (16-acre) plot by accident. 'The place is pretty much undiscovered, even by New Zealanders,' says Hay.

However, surrounded as it is by the typical topography of Great Barrier Island, the setting for the house is as magnificent as it is remote. Situated on a north-facing slope, at the point where the gradient changes from sloping hill to coastal flat, the house is tucked into the undulating pastures and native manuka bush that characterize the island's landscape. It overlooks a small cove, named after the surf break at its eastern tip – Shark Alley.

'The house is essentially an outdoor courtyard,' says Hay. 'It's set into the side of the hill and the resulting retaining terraces are used to nest the overall composition.' An L-shaped 'open veranda' contains the main living areas and runs around the edges of the courtyard, bounded only by enormous sliding glass doors on both sides.

'The advantage of the 2.5 metres (8 feet) wide by 2.7 metres (9 feet) high glass doors is that either side can be pulled closed to provide protection from the wind,' says Hay. 'With the prevailing weather coming from the sea, the windward side can provide shelter, leaving the leeward side open for access to the outdoor courtyard. The amount of glass used is an indicator of how special the view from the house really is.' With the doors left open, the whole house is exposed as an open pavilion, perched high on a rugged hill, spying on the Shark Alley surf as it pounds the little cove below.

'An outdoor courtyard'

Above Set into the side of a hill on this remote New Zealand island, this glass house can be exposed entirely to the elements.

Right Depending on the prevailing winds, the glazed sides can be closed for protection, or opened to welcome the breeze.

Left Aluminium storm shutters provide additional shelter.

Above The interior of the house is dominated by the ocean vista.

US: San Fernando Valley, California This minimalist glass house, perched on a ridge high above the San Fernando Valley of southern California, has been compared to the early Case Study designs – and it is easy to see why. The apparent simplicity of its construction and plentiful use of glass to bring in the view is certainly reminiscent of Pierre Koenig's Case Study 21, although it was built 50 years later in 2004 – coincidentally the year of Koenig's death.

Architect Zoltan E. Pali, of SPF:a created the home for a young couple who wanted to live as part of the landscape. To achieve this he made use of the transparency of glass to almost grab the scenery and drag it in. 'Glass was used as disappearing planes in the courtyards, as transparent view planes within the programmatic spaces and as light emitters in the clerestories,' explains Pali. 'We also threw in a few punched openings to maintain the clean shapes and forms.'

Although the house is arranged around a central spine, with independent access to living 'pods', with their own indoor-outdoor glass-walled courtyards, the main pull of the building is down the

Right This minimalist-style family home in southern California makes the most of floor-to-ceiling plate-glass windows and part-glazed courtyards to achieve the clients' dreams of capturing exterior space as living space, and harnessing the panoramic views of the San Fernando Valley.

Below Although the house has a very individual quality, many of the components were bought off-the-shelf.

'Living as part of the landscape'

Top left The house's sun terrace and infinity pool have a commanding view over the valley.

Left Large windows in the bedrooms mean the landscape is never out of sight.

Above The house is positioned in a shaded spot and its terraces make the most of the cooling breezes.

hillside and towards the floor-to-ceiling windows in the main living space. From here there is an uninterrupted view across a glass-like infinity swimming pool, which vanishes over the horizon on the site's northern edge and into the spectacular enormity of the valley beyond.

This is a house that is unquestionably at home in its environment because it works with the landscape, not only through the sensitivity of its design but also in how comfortably it sits in its location. Natural air-conditioning is provided by the positioning of the house on the land to take advantage of the shade, while the many courtyards make the most of the prevailing breezes.

Although the house has a distinctly bespoke feel, in fact many of the most arresting design features have been created through the imaginative use of standard materials. The aluminium edges that are such a feature of the building and help to frame the views, are in fact low-cost and off-the-shelf, further adding to this house's energy-conscious credentials and making sure that it impacts as little as possible on both the local and wider environments.

Brazil: Tijucopava This gleaming glass and white beach house has all the grace and grandeur of a high-class yacht moored on the lush shoreline at Tijucopava, Brazil. Built by São Paolo-based architect Isay Weinfeld in 1998, at the behest of a family that owns a Brazilian textile company, this is a house that is very much open to its environment, yet its owners were also keen to create something of a sense of mystery.

'There is an element of the unexpected here,' explains the practice's Mariana Nakiri. 'It was the owners' wish that the house had great integration between interior and exterior spaces, so we designed it to open both on to the garden and the swimming-pool deck, but from the front of the property all you can see is a tall wall that doesn't give a clue to what's behind it.'

In common with several of Weinfeld's other designs, the house is shielded from prying eyes by the high wall, which successfully conceals the house and creates a long and shaded corridor – the unassuming entrance to the property. At the end of the corridor, however, the building suddenly gives way to an enormous lawn and the front door. A tiny hallway is the first taste of the house, but this then explodes into the vast space of the main living area, with its 4.75-metre (16-foot) high ceilings and full-height glass doors, which pivot 90 degrees and open entirely to the swimming-pool deck and the breathtaking view.

'An element of the unexpected'

Left This glass and white beach house has a nautical quality, inside as well as out.

Right The long, narrow hallway, with its wood floor, shaded glazing and window seat has the atmosphere of a luxury liner.

The house is characterized by sleek glass panes on all three storeys, with views to the sea and the gardens. However, these are contrasted with materials of a variety of textures – rough as well as fine stucco, Portuguese mosaic stones, white pebbles and an aluminium curtain wall with electrostatic white painting.

Perched on the top of the house, and tracing the differing levels of its three floors, is a roof made up of wooden decks, which creates a peaceful place to contemplate the changing vista of the sea in this beautiful location.

Left, right and below As the 4.75-metre high glass panes pivot through ninety degrees, the cool, white living area is opened to the sun deck, with views of the gardens and the sea.

Chile: Tongoy 'Casa Klotz is a house that, despite its mass, is intended to appear transitory,' according to its Chilean architect, Mathias Klotz. 'This is why it is in an elevated position and its exterior gives the appearance of it being fragile and precarious.'

Built in 1991 as a holiday house overlooking a bay and a glorious stretch of beach in Tongoy, 400 kilometres (250 miles) north of Santiago, this rectangular wood and glass building certainly looks insubstantial and impermanent – more a refuge than a home. Inspired by the work of European modernists, in particular Marcel Breuer, Klotz's designs are very much centred on the human experience.

'The powerful contrast between the house and its surroundings is what defines the building,' says Klotz. It is a box 6 x 6 x 12 metres (20 x 20 x 40 feet), which sits upon the ground and rises 30 centimetres (12 inches) above it. The outside presents a blank face, which serves as the access over a curved bridge. The opposite façade, facing the sea, has large glazed openings.

The huge windows frame the view of the countryside to the rear and the sea to the front, and are accentuated by the fact that they are set in the untreated pine façade, which symbolizes Klotz's

'Intended to appear transitory'

Above and right A box made from untreated pine and great expanses of glass, according to its architect, this holiday home is little more than a basic shelter.

commitment to working with local materials and at the same time lends an unfinished look to the exterior of the building. 'The furniture and fittings are all basic,' says Klotz. 'They are reduced to just the things that are indispensable.'

The house's interior layout is very simple, with two clearly defined sections on the ground floor. The narrowest, 2 metres (6.5 feet) wide, is taken up with the entry, the stairs, the bathroom and a small bedroom, while the larger 4-metre (13-foot) wide space accommodates the main bedroom, the kitchen-dining area and the double-height living room. On the second floor, the bedrooms are set back from the sea-facing façade to create space for the terraces that give views over the bay.

Explains Klotz, 'The fine white carpentry, the openings in the wall, the added and subtracted features, the interplay between the proportions, the horizontal lines of the wooden sealing fillets on the façades are all touches aimed at producing a detailed close-up effect in contrast with the panorama of the surroundings and the abstraction of the building itself.'

Above The square panes, coupled with the very geometric design of the building are in contrast with the house's natural surroundings.

Above and left The house is just as unadorned on the inside as it is on the outside, with only minimal fittings and furnishings.

The Netherlands: Borneo Island, Amsterdam Architects Dick van Gameren and Bjarne Mastenbroek of De Architectengroep made the most of the opportunity to break free of the strict planning restrictions imposed on the urban regeneration of Borneo Island in Amsterdam.

Although the local planners had stipulated that the majority of new housing in the area should be at ground level, they conceded that this did not apply to buildings facing the open water. With this in mind, the architects set out to create a design for this block of 58 apartments that would offer a contrast to the mainly brick-built surrounding homes.

Abandoning the pattern of ground-level units this block, built in 1999, is a system of glass rooms, protected from general view by an overhanging terrace. In spite of the open character of the

'A seemingly impossible vantage point'

Left and below Free of the low-rise restrictions of their neighbours, these Dutch apartments enjoy spectacular views of the open water The end flats have the unique addition of a glass box living space that hangs out over the water for an astonishing 360-degree vista.

façades, the apartment building as a whole is fairly closed – in each apartment the bathroom and kitchen are housed in a central core, while the remainder of the living accommodation is open-plan and dominated by the large glazed windows. The overhanging terrace hides life in the apartment from the view of the street; at the same time, the largely transparent outer walls afford an unobstructed panoramic view of the water.

The most dramatic aspect of the design is in the stunning glass boxes that jut out from the end apartments and hang tantalizingly over the water. Reminiscent of Mies van der Rohe's Farnsworth House, these living spaces are transparent to the point of near invisibility. Totally surrounded by their environment, with stunning views from their seemingly impossible vantage point, these glass apartments offer a living experience that is very rare indeed.

Above Rectangular shafts of light permeate the glazed façade and fall on the clean white interior.

Above Reminiscent of the pure glass houses of the early Modernists, the living area of the end apartment is a simple glazed box, exposed to the setting.

Left Views of the water dominate the apartment at every turn.

Japan: Sagami Bay This striking glass home, on a dramatic stretch of Japanese coastline, is the result of a fusion of two traditions: the Japanese love of harmony and respect for nature, and the Western refinement of a dematerialized architecture of steel and glass. Designed by Foster+Partners in 1987, the house marked the start of an enduring relationship between the practice and the owners, which went on, through a series of further projects, to become an exploration of traditional Japanese architecture in a modern context.

Set on a raised platform, this house has a bird's-eye view of the volcanic coastline at Sagami Bay, not far from Tokyo, where

inaccessible fingers of lava jut out into the water. With the spectacular views central to the design, Foster+Partners created a steel-framed, glass-topped and glass-sided oblong, which welcomes in the views at every turn.

With the utility areas confined to the edges of the plan, the central section is left open as a flowing living space, dominated by expansive and breathtaking views of the rugged coastline and sea, which permeate the house through the full-height glazed sliding doors – the home's only boundary. The glass roof allows natural light to flood the space, but this can be tempered by adjustable louvres, which create striking shadow patterns depending on the time of day.

'The Japanese love of harmony and respect for nature'

Above This elegant, glass-sided oblong by Foster+Partners embodies both Japanese and Western architectural philosophies.

Left Simple full-height sliding doors reveal the tranquil rectangular pool and traditional landscaping.

Sliding screens can be used to subdivide the room as necessary, or alternatively the space can be opened up to embrace its setting as the glass doors slide open. Around the perimeter of the house are wooden terraces that allow the living area to be extended into the landscape, eroding the subtle division between inside and out.

With so much glass, the issue of privacy has been addressed by the planting of camphor trees to complement the mature trees on the cliff-top. A small teahouse of the late Edo period, brought from Shimane prefecture, cements the relationship of this contemporary glass house with its Japanese setting and tradition.

Left Full-height glazed sliding doors line the perimeter of this Japanese house, allowing the living spaces to open out on to adjoining terraces, eroding divisions between inside and out.

Below left The framed structure of the house creates seven rectangular bays defining the main spaces, which can be subdivided by means of sliding screens.

Right An obscured screen creates privacy in the glazed living area and bedroom.

US: Brentwood, California 'The house is a village of forms,' says LA-based architect Ed Niles of this curving glass edifice built in 1991 on top of a mountain in Brentwood, California for a local businessman and his family. 'Every form responds to a particular view that the client felt was important and, thanks to the superb location, there were several of them – the early morning view, the view of the city at night, the view from the living room to the ocean and the mountain views to the west.'

With so much spectacular scenery to capitalise on, Niles designed the house as a series of sleek, curving pavilions of blue-green tinted glass, with each room facing a different vista. 'The views are controlled,' says Niles, 'not just seen through a cut-out opening, they are reflections. The frame begins to control the view.'

As the Californian sun is angled low to the west, windows on that side of the house are kept to a minimum, while eighty-five per cent of the glass faces to the east and south, which is preferable for thermal mass. The expansive centrepiece dining room faces to the south and the city, while the master suite is flooded with the eastern sun. However, there was some concern about privacy on the western side, where the bathroom is sited, as it faces a built-up area in Mandeville Canyon. 'We had to go down into the valley and look up,' says Niles, 'then we knew to raise the glass to four feet in the shower area to preserve the owners' modesty.'

On the lower level, directly beneath the master suite, there is an office, as well as three children's bedrooms and a guest suite, all with stunning views of the mountains, while the house's impressive circular tower accommodates a living room and library.

'The high glass volume captures the ocean and the city at the same time,' says Niles, 'and also you can see the sculpture that is being made by the forms of the house itself.'

'A village of forms'

Right This highly original Californian glass house is described as 'a village of forms' by its architect. The circular tower accommodates the living room and library.

Left The sun glints on the pool as well as the curves of the glass, which has a slight blue-green tint and a low E coating to comply with California's very strict energy conservation rules.

Above The forms of the building frame the views of the city beyond.

Left Inside, vertical louvred blinds allow the sunlight to be controlled in the centrepiece dining area.

Right The master bedroom faces east and is flooded with sunlight.

Below A sweep of windows gives a panoramic view.

Spain: Montagut, Girona Designed for a young couple on a tight budget, Girona-based RCR Architects have created a sparkling, symmetrical glass home on an otherwise unprepossessing plot of Spanish countryside. Described by the architects as 'an insipid allotment', the one advantage of the site was its beautiful views and so these became the main focus of the construction.

A glass box, protected by a layer of metal mesh, was built in a workshop in 2000 and transported to the site in Montagut, Girona, where a semi-basement garage had already been excavated.

Although there are more contrasts than similarities, the shape of the house owes something to the design of a traditional country villa, with a symmetrical layout of two wings set on either side of a central section. The configuration of the internal spaces can be changed thanks to moveable panels that attach to the outside walls and alter the balance of the interior, from either three separate areas to one large, fluid space.

'The ever-changing moods of the landscape'

Right This sparkling glass box is a futuristic take on a traditional Spanish country house, with a central living and entertaining section supported by two wings of private accommodation.

Left Beneath the glazed house is a half-buried precinct that contains the garage.

Left The interior of the house can be reconfigured by moving the glass partitions.

Right Inside is dominated by the outside, and the changing Spanish landscape.

Below The glass wings of the house are visible from the main living space.

Areas for sleeping and study are provided for in the wings, while the main living space is in the central area – the glowing glass box – which, in its honest transparency, gives more than a nod to the seminal glass houses of Philip Johnson and Ludwig Mies van der Rohe. The simple, frameless clarity of this glass-sided living area puts on show the ordinary activities of daily life, with privacy provided only by the remoteness of the setting.

In common with both the Farnsworth House and Philip Johnson's Glass House, the pull of this Spanish glass house is to the outside, where the ever-changing moods of the landscape are reflected in the glass construction and brought inside to become an integral part of this futuristic re-imagining of a traditional country home.

US: Solano County, California 'The purpose of this house was to capture the views and pull them into the house as if they were an ever-changing work of art by nature,' says architect Helena Arahuete, who continues the practice of the highly influential John Lautner. And what views they are – this vantage point on the highest mountain in Solano County, California, next to the Napa wine region, is surrounded by a 360-degree panorama that takes in the Golden Gate Bridge in San Francisco as well the Sierra Nevada and Mount Diablo.

No wonder the owners spent many years tenaciously acquiring this extraordinary site. Tobacco-packaging entrepreneur John Roscoe and his wife Marilyn painstakingly bought the land in tiny parcels and, by 2003, when they had become the proud owners of 690 hectares (1,700 acres) of grassy hills and woods in this spectacular location, they determined to commission a building that would justify the beauty of its setting.

Before putting pencil to paper, Arahuete stood on the hilltop site and absorbed the surrounding landscape. The result is a home that is a stunning glass observatory, hexagonal in shape and simply styled to welcome in the landscape at every angle. The lower level is partly embedded into the hill and has two bedrooms, a library, an exercise room, utility rooms and a garage, but it is upstairs that the views really come to life. The top floor is largely open-plan, with only the master bedroom and bathrooms partitioned. The rest of the hexagon comprises the living, dining and kitchen areas, all

'A bird's-eye view'

Left This house is a stunning glass-sided hexagonal observatory, designed by John Lautner. Its tapered roofs of varied heights give the impression of lightness.

Above Perched on the top of one of California's highest mountains, the house has 360-degree views of the Sierra Nevada and San Francisco.

dominated by the dramatic valleys all around, which seem close enough to touch through the full-height frameless plate-glass windows.

With a bird's-eye view of its spectacular surroundings, and such a light footprint, this house is very much at home in its environment. Externally, it is almost transparent, and certainly hard to pick out from a distance. Tapered roofs give the illusion of weightlessness, and the different ceiling heights disguise the fact that the internal space is enormous, with the expansive views barely interrupted by internal supports and beams.

Although the house is certainly visually connected to the landscape, there is also a physical bridge in the shape of the Roscoes's swimming pool. Unable to choose between an indoor and an outdoor pool, Arahuete presented the couple with one that passes beneath the glass wall of the house, allowing the owners of this spectacular home the chance not just to look at their environment, but to glide effortlessly into it, too.

Above A sweeping outdoor staircase leads from the top storey to the lower level.

Right The swimming pool moves fluently from inside to outside, passing beneath the glass wall of the house.

Opposite Frameless windows pull in the spectacular view and swivel open to reveal the living space to the environment.

Following pages The stunning hanging pool leads out into the dramatic landscape.

Left The dining space, with its stone floor and natural wood ceiling, is a fabulous vantage point.

Below On the top floor, the master bedroom has superb panoramic views through full-height plate glass windows.

Indonesia: Tukad Balean, Bal Set on a former paddy field in Tukad Balean in the Bal province of Indonesia, this strikingly linear glass house was designed by local architects Antony Liu and Ferry Ridwan in response to the longing of their client, a landscape gardener, for a home that would be 'simple and harmonious with its landscape' and 'oriented to nature'.

Designed to be a highly private home and office for the owner and his family, the house was also required to retain some flexibility, so that the most beautiful aspects of the landscape could be appreciated at different times of the day and the year. The client was adamant that not a single tree should be 'killed', because 'through the trees, nature will appear as it is'. The result is a residence that is almost a part of the landscape itself, with seemingly insubstantial boundaries. As most of the natural trees have been retained, the setting is very natural, and the building itself has been constructed to tread extremely lightly on its environment.

The very elongated design allows for great expanses of glass sliding doors that can be opened to allow fresh air to permeate the building and to completely erode the boundaries between inside and out. Wooden latticed insect screens also create a permeable outer skin to the building, and the solid exterior walls are finished in a soft plaster that captures the shadows of the movement of the trees as they blow in the breeze.

A long pool, set to one side of the house, connects the views of the master bedroom, living room, and children's bedrooms and forms a bond with the natural elements of the home's beautiful surroundings.

Above As the building is in two parts – one the owner's office and the other his home – a series of pivoting obscured glass doors is used to divide or bring together the two areas as necessary.

Above In the words of its architect, this linear glass house is 'simple and harmonious with its landscape'.

'A bond with the natural elements'

Above Sliding glass doors in the kitchen allow the space to be opened to the environment.

Above The sloping ceiling in the living area creates an angled space above the partition wall, allowing the air to flow freely.

Left The bedroom is dominated by views of the setting, once a paddy field.

Conclusion

With so many spectacular glass houses already in existence, and many more biding their time on the drawing boards of architects' offices all over the world, it is hard to imagine that the future of residential architecture will not be highlighted with ever-more daring, original and beautiful homes made of glass.

Just as the seminal glass houses of the 20th century have provided a wealth of innovative ideas for the glass architects of today, the sparkling homes that fill the pages of this book will certainly serve as a source of inspiration for those who are yet to pick up their pencils. And, if the technological advances in glass manufacture achieved over the past century are anything to go by, the next 100 years will surely provide architects with an increasingly versatile transparent building material that will stretch their creativity even further.

Improvements to the thermal properties of glass – as well as to its potential for bearing loads and remaining tough and safe even at enormous proportions – will offer architects the means to imagine, design and construct glass houses that are increasingly practical and pleasurable to live in, while at the same time stunning and spectacular to look at. Glass houses have a fabulous future. Clearly.

Directory of Architects

Barton Myers Associates
T. +1 310 208 2227
www.bartonmyers.com

Stéphane Beel Architecten
T. +32 09 269 51 50
www.stephanebeel.com

Belsize Architects
T. +44 (0)20 7482 4420
www.belsizearchitects.com

Lynn Davis Architects
T. +44 (0)1304 612089

Terry Farrell and Partners
T. +44 (0)20 7258 3433
www.terryfarrell.co.uk

Fearon Hay
T. +64 9 309 0128
www.fearonhay.co.nz

Lee Fitzgerald Architects
T +44 (0)20 7089 6440
www.leefitzgeraldarchitects.co.uk

Foster & Partners
T. +44 (0)20 7738 0455
www.fosterandpartners.com

Kenneth E. Hobgood Architects
T. +1 919 8287711
www.kennethhobgood.com

Eva Jiricna
T. +44 (0)20 7554 2400
www.ejal.com

Stephen Kanner
T. +1 310 451 5400
www.kannerarch.com

Mathias Klotz
T. +56 2 676 2701
www.mathiasklotz.com

Marcio Kogan
T. +55 11 3081 3522
www.marciokogan.com.br

Lautner Associates
T. +1 310 577 7783
www.lautnerassociates.com

Antony Liu
T +62 816 810 691
Email tonton@dnet.net.id

Daniel Marshall Architect
T. +64 09 3023661
www.marshall-architect.co.nz

David Mikhail
T. +44 (0)20 7377 8424
www.davidmikhail.com

Munkenbeck & Marshall
T. +44 (0)20 7739 3300
www.mandm.uk.com

Edward R. Niles Architect
T. +1 310 457 3602
www.ednilesarchitect.com

RCR Arquitectes
T. +34 972 269 105
www.rcrarquitectes.es

Richard Rogers Partnership
T. +44 (0)20 7385 1235
www.richardrogers.co.uk

Harry Seidler
T. +61 2 99221388
www.seidler.net.au

SPF Architects
T. +1 310 558 0902
www.spfa.com

Seth Stein
T. +44 (0)20 8968 8581
www.sethstein.com

Dick van Gameren & Bjarne Mastenbroek – de Architectengroep
T +31 020 530 4850

Vincens & Ramos Arquitects
T. +34 915210004

Isay Weinfeld
T. +55 11 3079 7581
www.isayweinfeld.com

Picture Credits

Front Cover

House in Kensington: London, Richard Bryant/arcaid

Back Cover

Indonesia: Tukad Balean, Bal, Sonny Sandjaya/arcaid.

1 John Edward Linden/arcaid
4-5 Richard Bryant/arcaid
6-7 Alan Weintraub/arcaid

Chapter 1: The Innovators

10 Case Study House, John Edward Linden/arcaid
12-15 UK: Chertsey Surrey, Richard Bryant/arcaid
16 US: Canaan, Connecticut, Bill Marris/Esto/arcaid
17 US: Canaan, Connecticut, Richard Bryant/arcaid
18-21 US: Plano, Illinois, Alan Wentraub/arcaid
22-25 US: Hollywood Hills, California, John Edward Linden/arcaid
26-27 Australia: Wahroonga, NSW, Richard Bryant/arcaid
28-31 UK: East Grinstead, Surrey, Richard Bryant/arcaid
32-35 UK: Wimbledon, London, Richard Bryant/arcaid

Chapter 2: Indoor-Outdoor Living

36 Brazil: São Paulo, Alan Weintraub/arcaid
38-41 US: Pacific Palisades, California, John Edward Linden/arcaid
42-45 US: Montecito, California, Richard Powers/arcaid
46-49 Brazil: Rio de Janeiro, Alan Weintraub/arcaid
50-53 Brazil: São Paulo, Alan Weintraub/arcaid
54-57 UK: Petersham, London, Richard Bryant/arcaid
58-63 US: Malibu, California, John Edward Linden/arcaid
64-67 UK: Highgate, London, Nicholas Kane/arcaid
68-71 NZ: Waitemata Harbour, Auckland, Richard Powers/arcaid
72-77 UK: Hammersmith, London, Richard Bryant/arcaid
78-81 UK: Deal, Kent, Richard Bryant/arcaid
82-85 Canada, Toronto, Richard Bryant/arcaid
86-89 US: Bel Air, California, John Edward Linden/arcaid
90-95 Ibiza, Spain, Eugeni Pons/arcaid

Chapter 3: Breathing New Life

96 UK: Kensington, London, Richard Bryant/arcaid
98-101 UK: Chelsea, London, Richard Bryant/arcaid
102-105 UK: Camden, London, Richard Bryant/arcaid
106-109 UK: Stockwell, London, Nicholas Kane/arcaid
110-113 UK: Highgate, London, Richard Bryant/arcaid
114-119 US: Los Angeles, California, Alan Weintraub/arcaid
120-123 UK: Kensington, London, Richard Bryant/arcaid
124-127 US: Charlotte, North Carolina, Paul Warchol/archenova/arcaid

Chapter 4: At Home in the Landscape

128-133 Brazil: Rio de Janeiro, Alan Weintraub/arcaid
134-139 France: Cap Ferrat, Richard Bryant/arcaid
140-143 Belgium: West Flanders, Alberto Piovano/arcaid
144-147 New Zealand: Great Barrier Island, Richard Powers/arcaid
148-151 US: San Fernando Valley, California, John Edward Linden/arcaid
152-155 Brazil: Tijucopava, Alan Weintraub/arcaid
156-159 Chile: Tongoy, Alberto Piovano/arcaid
160-163 Netherlands: Borneo Island, Amsterdam, Nicholas Kane/arcaid
164-167 Japan: Sagami Bay, Ian Lambot/arcaid
168-173 US: Brentwood, California, Alan Weintraub/arcaid
174-177 Spain: Montagut, Girona, Eugeni Pons/arcaid
178-185 US: Solano County, California, Alan Weintraub/arcaid
186-189 Indonesia: Tukad Balean, Bal, Sonny Sandjaya/arcaid

For further information about the work of photographers featured in this book go to: www.arcaid.co.uk

Acknowledgements

Huge thanks to Colin Webb and Victoria Webb at Palazzo Editions, as well as Bernard Higton, Catherine Hooper and Sonya Newland for their major roles in the making of this book, and particularly to Sue Ucel at Arcaid Image Library whose help has been invaluable. More thanks to Richard, Lucy and Charley for their very welcome support, and of course to all the architects who gave up their time to tell me about their incredible glass houses.
Nicky Adams, June 2007